Business Vocabulary in Use

Bill Mascull

CAMBRIDGE
UNIVERSITY PRESS

CAMBRIDGE UNIVERSITY PRESS
Cambridge, New York, Melbourne, Madrid, Cape Town, Singapore, São Paulo

Cambridge University Press
The Edinburgh Building, Cambridge CB2 8RU, UK

www.cambridge.org
Information on this title: www.cambridge.org/9780521775298

First published 2002
10th printing 2007

Printed in Dubai by Oriental Press

A catalogue record for this publication is available from the British Library

ISBN 978-0-521-77529-8

Contents

FINANCE AND THE ECONOMY

DOING THE RIGHT THING

PERSONAL SKILLS

Introduction

Who is this book for?

Business Vocabulary in Use is designed to help intermediate and upper-intermediate learners of business English improve their business vocabulary. It is for people studying English before they start work and for those already working who need English in their job.

Apart from improving your business vocabulary, the book also helps you to develop the language needed for important business communication skills.

You can use the book on your own for self-study, or with a teacher in the classroom, one-to-one or in groups.

How is the book organised?

The book has 66 two-page units.

The first 47 of these units are **thematic** and look at the vocabulary of business areas such as people, organisations, production, marketing, finance and business-related economics.

The other 19 units focus on the language of **skills** you need in business, such as those for presentations, meetings, telephoning and negotiations.

The left-hand page of each unit explains new words and expressions, and the right-hand page allows you to check and develop your understanding of them and how they are used through a series of exercises.

There is **cross-referencing** between units to show connections between the same word or similar words used in different contexts.

There is an **answer key** at the back of the book. Most of the exercises have questions with only one correct answer. But some of the exercises, including the **Over to you** activities at the end of each section (see below), are designed for writing and/or discussion about yourself and your own organisation.

There is also an **index**. This lists all the new words and phrases introduced in the book and gives the unit numbers where they appear. The index also tells you how the words and expressions are pronounced.

The left-hand page

This page introduces new vocabulary and expressions for each thematic or skills area. The presentation is divided into a number of sections indicated by letters: A, B, C, etc, with simple, clear titles.

As well as explanations of vocabulary, there is information about typical word combinations and the grammar associated with particular vocabulary, for example the verbs that are typically used with particular nouns.

There are notes on mistakes to avoid, for example:

- ■ You can't say that someone is 'a responsible'.

There are also notes about differences between British and American English.

- ■ BrE: CV; AmE: résumé or resume

The right-hand page

The exercises on the right-hand page give practice in using the new vocabulary and expressions presented on the left-hand page. Sometimes the exercises concentrate on using the words or expressions presented on the left-hand page in context. Other exercises practise the grammatical forms of items from the left-hand page. Some units contain diagrams to complete, or crosswords.

'Over to you' sections

An important feature of *Business Vocabulary in Use* is the **Over to you** section at the end of each unit. There are sometimes alternative **Over to you** sections, for learners who are in work and those who are not. The **Over to you** sections give you the chance to put into practice the words and expressions in the unit in relation to your own professional situation, studies or opinions.

Self-study learners can do this section as a written activity.

In the classroom, the **Over to you** sections can be used as the basis for discussion with the whole class, or in small groups with a spokesperson for each group summarising the discussion and its outcome for the class. The teacher can then get students to look again at the exercises relating to points that have caused difficulty. Students can follow up by using the **Over to you** section as a written activity, for example as homework.

How to use the book for self-study

Find the topic you are looking for by referring to the contents page or the index. Read through the explanations on the left-hand page of the unit. Do the exercises on the right-hand page. Check your answers in the key. If you have made some mistakes, go back and look at the explanations and exercise again. Note down important words and expressions in your notebook.

How to use the book in the classroom

Teachers can choose units that relate to students' particular needs and interests, for example areas they have covered in course books, or that have come up in other activities. Alternatively, lessons can contain a regular vocabulary slot, where students look systematically at the vocabulary of particular thematic or skills areas.

Students can work on the units in pairs, with the teacher going round the class assisting and advising. Teachers should get students to think about the logical process of the exercises, pointing out why one answer is possible and others are not.

We hope you enjoy using this book.

1 Work and jobs

A What do you do?

To find out what someone's job is you say **'What do you do?'** Here, Kerstin talks about her job:

'I **work for** a large European car maker. I **work on** car design. In fact, I **run** the design department and I **manage** a team of designers: 20 people **work under** me. It's very interesting. One of my main **responsibilities** is to make sure that new model designs are finished on time. I'm also **in charge of** design budgets.

I **deal with** a lot of different people in the company. I'm **responsible for** co-ordination between design and production: I **work with** managers at our manufacturing plants.'

Note:

$$\left.\begin{array}{l}\textbf{in charge of} \\ \textbf{responsible for}\end{array}\right\} + \begin{array}{l}\text{noun} \\ \text{verb + -ing}\end{array}$$

responsibility + infinitive or -ing
    One of my responsibilities is to make sure ...
    One of my responsibilities is making sure ...

 You can't say ~~I'm a responsible~~.

B Word combinations with 'work'

If you **work** or **have work**, you have a job. But you don't say that someone has ~~a work~~. **Work** is also the place where you do your job.

Here are some phrases with 'work':

- Hi, I'm Frank. I work in a bank in New York City. I **leave for work** at 7.30 every morning.
- I **go to work** by train and subway.
- I **get to / arrive at work** at about nine.
- I'm usually **at work** till six.
- Luckily, I don't get ill very much so I'm not often **off work**.

The economy is growing fast and more people are **in work** than ever before. The percentage of people **out of work** has fallen to its lowest level for 30 years.

 You don't say, for example, ~~I'm at the work~~ or ~~I'm going to the work~~.

C Types of job and types of work

A **full-time job** is for the whole of the normal working week; a **part-time job** is for less time than that.

You say that someone **works full-time** or **part-time**.

A **permanent job** does not finish after a fixed period; a **temporary job** finishes after a fixed period.

You talk about **temporary work** and **permanent work**.

1.1 Pierre is talking about his work. Correct what he says.

I work for a French supermarket company. (1) I work *about* the development of new supermarkets. (2) In fact, I *running* the development department and (3) I *am manage for* a team looking at the possibilities in different countries. It's very interesting. (4) One of my *main* is to make sure that new supermarkets open on time. (5) I'm also *charged with* financial reporting. (6) I deal *at* a lot of different organizations in my work. (7) I'm *responsible of* planning projects from start to finish. (8) I work closely *near* our foreign partners, and so I travel a lot.

1.2 Complete the text with one of the prepositions from B opposite.

Rebecca lives in London and works in public relations. She leaves home for work at 7.30 am. She drives (1) .... work. The traffic is often bad and she worries about getting (2) .... work late, but she usually arrives (3) .... work at around nine. She finishes work quite late, at about eight. 'Luckily, I'm never ill,' she says. 'I could never take the time (4) .... work.'

She loves what she does and is glad to be (5) .... work. Some of her friends are not so lucky: they are (6) .... work.

1.3 Write about each person using words from C opposite, and the words in brackets. The first one has been done for you.

1 I'm Alicia. I work in a public library in the afternoons from two until six. (I/job)
   I have a part-time job.
2 My husband works in an office from 9 am to 5.30 pm. (he/job)
3 Our daughter works in a bank from eight till five every day. (she/work)
4 I'm David and I work in a café from 8 pm until midnight. (I/work)
5 My wife works in local government and she can have this job for as long as she wants it. (she/job)
6 Our son is working on a farm for four weeks. (he/job)
7 Our daughter is working in an office for three weeks. (she/work)

Over to you

If you work ...

What do you do? What are you in charge of? What are your responsibilities?

What time do you leave for work? How long does it take you to get to work? What time do you arrive at work? Do you take a lot of time off work?

If you don't work ...

What sort of job would you like to do?

What routine would you like to have?

2 Ways of working

A Old and new ways

I'm an **office worker** in an insurance company. It's a **nine-to-five** job with regular **working hours**. The work isn't very interesting, but I like to be able to go home at a reasonable time.

We all have to **clock in** and **clock out** every day. In this company, even the managers have to, which is unusual!

Note: You also say **clock on** and **clock off**.

I'm in computer programming. There's a system of **flexitime** in my company, which means we can work when we want, within certain limits. We can start at any time before eleven, and finish as early as three, as long as we do enough hours each month. It's ideal for me as I have two young children.

BrE: flexitime
AmE: flextime

I work in a car plant. I work in **shifts**. I may be on the **day shift** one week and the **night shift** the next week. It's difficult changing from one shift to another. When I change shifts, I have problems changing to a new routine for sleeping and eating.

I'm a commercial artist in an advertising agency. I work in a big city, but I prefer living in the country, so I **commute** to work every day, like thousands of other **commuters**. **Working from home** using a computer and the Internet is becoming more and more popular, and the agency is introducing this: it's called **teleworking** or **telecommuting**. But I like going into the office and working with other people around me.

Teleworking   Clocking in

B Nice work if you can get it

All these words are used in front of 'job' and 'work':

- **satisfying, stimulating, fascinating, exciting**: the work is interesting and gives you positive feelings.
- **dull, boring, uninteresting, unstimulating**: the work is not interesting.
- **repetitive, routine**: the work involves doing the same things again and again.
- **tiring, tough, hard, demanding**: the work is difficult and makes you tired.

C Nature of work

My work involves ...

+ noun
human contact
long hours
team work

+ -ing
solving problems
travelling a lot
dealing with customers

2.1 Which person (1–5) is most likely to do each of the five things (a–e)?

1 A software designer in an Internet company. Has to be in the office.
2 An office worker in a large, traditional manufacturing company.
3 A manager in a department store in a large city. Lives in the country.
4 A construction worker on a building site where work goes on 24 hours a day.
5 A technical writer for a city computer company. Lives in the country.

a work in shifts
b work under a flexitime system
c telecommute
d commute to work
e clock on and off at the same time every day

2.2 Look at the words and expressions in B and C opposite.
Five people talk about their jobs. Match the jobs (1–5) to the people (a–e)
and put the words in brackets into the correct grammatical forms.

1 accountant
2 postwoman
3 flight attendant
4 software developer
5 teacher

a Obviously, my work involves .... (travel) a lot. It can be quite
physically .... (tire), but I enjoy .... (deal) with
customers, except when they become violent. Luckily this doesn't happen often.

b I like .... (work) with figures, but my job is much less .... (bore)
and routine than people think. The work .... (involve) a lot of human
contact and teamwork, working with other managers.

c Of course, it involves getting up quite early in the morning. But I like
.... (be) out in the open air. And I get a lot of exercise!

d You've got to think in a very logical way. The work can be mentally
.... (tire), but it's very satisfying to write a program that works.

e I love my job. It's very .... (stimulate) and not at all
.... (repeat): no two days are the same. It's good to see the children
learn and develop.

Over to you

If you work ...

Do you have a nine-to-five job?
Do you have to clock on and off? Is there
a flexitime system in your organization?
Are there people who do shiftwork in
your company?

Could you do your job working from
home? If so, would you like to?

If you don't work ...

What sort of working hours would you
like to have if you worked?

Would you like to work from home?

3 Recruitment and selection

A Recruitment

The process of finding people for particular jobs is **recruitment** or, especially in American English, **hiring**. Someone who has been recruited is a **recruit** or, in American English, a **hire**. The company **employs** or **hires** them; they **join** the company. A company may recruit employees directly or use outside **recruiters**, **recruitment agencies** or **employment agencies**. Outside specialists called **headhunters** may be called on to **headhunt** people for very important jobs, persuading them to leave the organizations they already work for. This process is called **headhunting**.

B Applying for a job

Fred is a van driver, but he was fed up with long trips. He looked in the **situations vacant** pages of his local newspaper, where a local supermarket was advertising for van drivers for a new delivery service. He **applied for** the job by completing an **application form** and sending it in.

Harry is a building engineer. He saw a job in the **appointments** pages of one of the national papers. He made an application, sending in his **CV** (**curriculum vitae** – the 'story' of his working life) and a **covering letter** explaining why he wanted the job and why he was the right person for it.

Note: **Situation**, **post** and **position** are formal words often used in job advertisements and applications.

> BrE: **CV**; AmE: **résumé or resume**
> BrE: **covering letter**; AmE: **cover letter**

C Selection procedures

Dagmar Schmidt is the head of recruitment at a German telecommunications company. She talks about the **selection process**, the methods that the company uses to recruit people:

A job interview

'We advertise in national newspapers. We look at the **backgrounds** of **applicants**: their **experience** of different jobs and their educational **qualifications**. We don't ask for handwritten **letters of application** as people usually apply by email; **handwriting analysis** belongs to the 19th century.

We invite the most interesting **candidates** to a **group discussion**. Then we have individual **interviews** with each candidate. We also ask the candidates to do written **psychometric tests** to assess their intelligence and personality.

After this, we **shortlist** three or four candidates. We check their **references** by writing to their **referees**: previous employers or teachers that candidates have named in their applications. If the references are OK, we ask the candidates to come back for more interviews. Finally, we **offer** the job to someone, and if they **turn it down** we have to think again. If they **accept** it, we **hire** them. We only **appoint** someone if we find the right person.'

3.1 Complete the crossword. Use appropriate forms of words from A, B and C opposite.

Across

5 I phoned to check on my application, but they said they'd already .... someone. (9)

6 This job is so important, I think we need to .... someone. (8)

8 The selection process has lasted three months, but we're going to .... someone next week. (7)

Down

1 and 2 I hope she ...., because if she .... the job, we'll have to start looking again. (7,5,4)

3 That last applicant was very strong, but I understand he's had two other .... already. (6)

4 They've finally .... a new receptionist. (5)

7 Computer programmers wanted. Only those with UNIX experience should ....(5)

3.2 Now divide the words in 3.1 into two groups:
1 what a company personnel department does.
2 what a person looking for work does.

3.3 Replace the underlined phrases with correct forms of words and expressions from A, B and C opposite.

Fred had already (1) <u>refused</u> two job offers when he went for (2) <u>a discussion to see if he was suitable</u> for the job. They looked at his driving licence and contacted (3) <u>previous employers Fred had mentioned in his application</u>. A few days later, the supermarket (4) <u>asked him if he would like the job</u> and Fred (5) <u>said yes</u>.

Harry didn't hear anything for six weeks, so he phoned the company. They told him that they had received a lot of (6) <u>requests for the job</u>. After looking at the (7) <u>life stories</u> of the (8) <u>people asking for the job</u> and looking at (9) <u>what exams they had passed during their education</u>, the company (10) <u>had chosen six people to interview, done tests on their personality and intelligence</u> and they had then given someone the job.

Over to you

If you work ...

How did you get your job? Was it advertised? Were you interviewed for it? Was the selection process very long?

If you don't work ...

Have you applied for any jobs? Were you interviewed? How did it go? What's the usual process for getting your first job in your country?

4 Skills and qualifications

A Education and training

Graduates

In AmE, you also say that someone **graduates** from high school (the school that people usually leave when they are 18).

Margareta: The trouble with **graduates**, people who've just left university, is that their **paper qualifications** are good, but they have no **work experience**. They just don't know how business works.

Nils: I disagree. **Education** should teach people how to think, not prepare them for a particular job. One of last year's recruits had **graduated from** Oxford in philosophy and she's doing very well!

Margareta: Philosophy's an interesting subject, but for our company, it's more useful if you **train as** a scientist and **qualify as** a biologist or chemist – **training for** a specific job is better.

Nils: Yes, but we don't just need scientists. We also need good managers, which we can achieve through **in-house training** courses within the company. You know we have put a lot of money into **management development** and **management training** because they are very important. You need to have some management experience for that. It's not the sort of thing you can learn when you're 20!

B Skilled and unskilled

A **skill** is the ability to do something well, especially because you have learned how to do it and practised it.

Jobs, and the people who do them, can be described as:

highly skilled	**skilled**	**semi-skilled**	**unskilled**
(e.g. car designer)	(e.g. car production manager)	(e.g. taxi driver)	(e.g. car cleaner)

You can say that someone is:

skilled at,
or skilled in ...

+ noun
customer care
electronics
computer software

+ -ing
communicating
using PCs
working with large groups

You can also say that someone is:

good with ...

computers
figures
people

C The right person

These words are often used in job advertisements. Companies look for people who are:

- **self-starters, proactive, self-motivated,** or **self-driven:** good at working on their own.
- **methodical, systematic** and **organized:** can work in a planned, orderly way.
- **computer-literate:** good with computers.
- **numerate:** good with numbers.
- **motivated:** very keen to do well in their job.
- **talented:** naturally very good at what they do.
- **team players:** people who work well with other people.

4.1 Correct these sentences about Ravi, using words from A opposite. One word is wrong in each item.

1 At 18, Ravi decided to stay in full-time *training* and went to Mumbai University.
2 Ravi *qualified* three years later with a degree in philosophy and politics.
3 He taught for a while, but didn't like it. He decided to *educate* as an accountant at evening classes.
4 He qualified *for* an accountant and joined a big accountancy firm in its Mumbai office.
5 When he started, he needed to develop other skills, which would come through *experiments*.
6 He received *managers'* training to help him develop these skills.

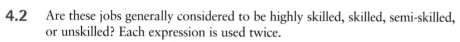

4.2 Are these jobs generally considered to be highly skilled, skilled, semi-skilled, or unskilled? Each expression is used twice.

1 teacher
2 brain surgeon
3 car worker on a production line
4 airline pilot
5 office cleaner
6 labourer (someone doing basic work on a building site)
7 bus driver
8 office manager

4.3 Complete these extracts from job advertisements using words from C opposite.

1 You'll need to be _ _ _ _ _ _ _ _ , as you'll be working on financial budgets.

4 We need _ _ _ _ _ _ _ _ journalists who are very good at their job and extremely _ _ _ _ _ _ _ _ _ to find out as much as they can.

2 As part of our sales team, you'll be working independently, so you have to be self-_ _ _ _ _ _ _ _ _ and self-_ _ _ _ _ _ .

3 We're looking for someone who can work on ten projects at once. You must be _ _ _ _ _ _ _ _ _ _ , _ _ _ _ _ _ _ _ _ _ and _ _ _ _ _ _ _ _ _ _ .

5 You'll be researching developments on the Internet, so you have to be _ _ _ _ _ _ _ _ - _ _ _ _ _ _ _ _ . You must be _ _ _ _ _ _ _ _ _ , able to work on your own initiative, and a _ _ _ _ - _ _ _ _ _ _ _ _ . But as part of a team of researchers, you need to be a good _ _ _ _ - _ _ _ _ _ _ too.

Over to you

If you work ...

What sort of people does your organization look for in its recruitment? What sort of person are you?

If you don't work ...

Does your educational institution prepare people for specific jobs?

5 Pay and benefits

A Wages, salary and benefits

My name's Luigi and I'm a hotel manager in Venice. I get paid a **salary** every month. In summer we're very busy, so we work a lot of extra hours, or **overtime**; the money for this is quite good. Working in a hotel, we also get nice **perks**, for example free meals!

I'm Ivan and I work as a waiter in Prague. I like my job even if I don't **earn** very much: I get paid **wages** every week by the restaurant. We get the **minimum wage**: the lowest amount allowed by law. But we also get **tips**, money that customers leave for us in addition to the bill. Some tourists are very generous!

I'm Catherine and I'm a saleswoman based in Paris. I get a **basic salary**, plus **commission**: a percentage on everything I sell. If I sell more than a particular amount in a year, I also get extra money – a **bonus**, which is nice. There are some good **fringe benefits** with this job: I get a **company car**, and they make payments for my **pension**, money that I'll get regularly after I stop working. All that makes a good **benefits package**.

B Compensation 1

My name's Alan. I'm a specialist in **pay** and **benefits**. **Compensation** and **remuneration** are formal words used to talk about pay and benefits, especially those of senior managers. **Compensation package** and **remuneration package** are used especially in the US to talk about all the pay and benefits that employees receive. For a senior executive, this may include **share options** (BrE) or **stock options** (AmE): the right to buy the company's shares at low prices. (See Unit 36) There may be **performance-related bonuses** if the manager reaches particular objectives for the company.

C Compensation 2

Compensation is also used to talk about money and other benefits that a senior manager (or any employee) receives if they are forced to leave the organization, perhaps after a **boardroom row**. This money is in the form of a **compensation payment**, or **severance payment**. If the manager also receives benefits, the payment and the benefits form a **severance package**.

In Britain, executives with very high pay and good benefits may be referred to as **fat cats**, implying that they do not deserve this level of remuneration.

5.1 Xavier and Yvonne are talking about Xavier's new job as a photocopier salesman. Complete the conversation, using words from A opposite.

1 X: I get paid every month.

   Y: I see. You get a salary , not wages.

2 X: I usually have to work late: I don't get paid for it, but I get a percentage for every photocopier I sell.

   Y: So you don't get .... , but you do get .... That's good.

3 X: The people in production get a .... if they reach their targets.

   Y: Oh right. They get an extra payment for producing a certain amount.

4 X: The company pays for medical treatment too, and the company restaurant is fantastic.

   Y: Wow! The .... sound very nice.

5 X: And they've given me a .... to go and visit clients.

   Y: So you don't have to buy a car, then.

6 X: What's more, the company pays in money for us to get when we don't work any more.

   Y: Yes, it's important to get a good ....

7 X: The total .... is brilliant.

   Y: Yes, all that extra stuff is really worth having.

5.2 Which expressions from B and C opposite could be used to continue each of these newspaper extracts?

1

FAILED AIRLINE BOSS GETS MASSIVE PAYOUT

Shareholders are angry that despite very poor results, Blighty Airlines' CEO, Mr Rob Herring, is leaving with £3 million in his pocket. They say it is ridiculous to 'reward' bad performance with this sort of …

(2 possible expressions)

3

MEGAFONE CEO GETS £10 MILLION 'THANK YOU' AFTER TAKEOVER

The directors of Megafone, the world's largest mobile phone company, yesterday voted to give Mr Chris Ladyman, its chief executive, a special payment of £10 mil-lion for negotiating the company's takeover of Minnemann. The directors referred to this as a …

(1 possible expression)

2

MULTILEVER'S EXECUTIVE PAY

It was today revealed that Mr Carl Lang, head of consumer foods giant Multilever, earns a basic salary of $22 million with stock options potentially worth an additional $10 million. Other payments bring to $35 million his total …

(2 possible expressions)

4

ANGRY SHAREHOLDERS ATTACK EXECUTIVE PAY

National Energy's shareholders yesterday attacked the directors of the company for paying themselves too much. Profits fell by 30 per cent last year, but directors are being paid 30 per cent more. 'They should be paid 30 per cent less,' said one shareholder. 'These people are just …'

(1 possible expression)

 Over to you

Do you think top executives are too highly paid? Or do they deserve what they earn?

6 People and workplaces

Employees and management

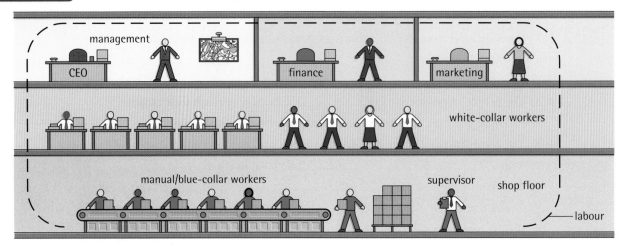

The people who work for a company, all the people on its **payroll**, are its **employees, personnel, staff, workers** or **workforce**. But these words can mean just the people carrying out the work of a company, rather than those leading it and organizing it: the **management**.

Note: **Workforce, work-force** and **work force** are all possible.

B Management and administration

A company's activities may be spread over different **sites**. A company's most senior managers usually work in its **head office** or **headquarters** (HQ). Some managers have their own individual **offices**, but in many businesses, most employees work in **open-plan offices**: large areas where many people work together. Administration or, informally, admin, the everyday work supporting a company's activities, is often done in offices like these by **administrative staff** or **support staff**. For example, those giving technical help to buyers of the company's products are in **technical support**.

An open-plan office

C Labour

Labour is spelled **labor** in AmE. **Labor unions**, organizations defending the interests of workers (AmE) are called **trade unions** in BrE.

When workers are not happy with pay or conditions, they may take **industrial action**:

- a **strike, stoppage** or **walk-out**: workers stop working for a time.
- a **go-slow**: workers continue to work, but more slowly than usual.
- an **overtime ban**: workers refuse to work more than the normal number of hours.

D Personnel and human resources

In larger organizations there is a **human resources department** (HRD) that deals with pay, recruitment, etc. This area is called **human resources** (HR) or **human resource management** (HRM). Another name for this department is the **personnel department**.

6.1 Look at A, B and C opposite to find the answers to the crossword.

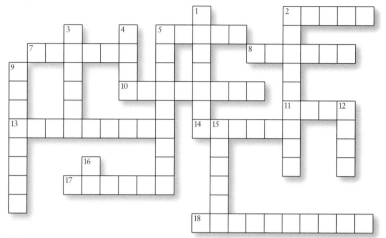

Across

2 and 17 Office workers may wear this. (5,6)

5 All the people working for a company. (5)

7 .... workers use their hands. (6)

8 When people stop working to protest. (6)

10 One of the people working for an organization. (8)

11 Occasions when workers stop working to protest: walk-............ (4)

13 Another name for the human resources department. (9)

14 Workers seen as a group. (6)

18 and 15 down Various forms of protest at work. (10,6)

Down

1 Everyone working for a company is on this. (7)

2 Everyone, or everyone except top managers. (9)

3 These are trade in the UK and labor in the US. (6)

4 and 17 across Manual workers may wear this. (4,6)

5 The place in a factory where the production lines are. (4, 5)

9 When people stop work to complain about something. (8)

16 and 12 When workers intentionally produce less. (2,4)

6.2 Manuel Ortiz is the founder of a Spanish computer sales company. Use the words in B and D opposite to complete what he says about it.

I founded Computadoras Creativas 20 years ago. We started with a small

(1) _ _ _ _ _ _ in Madrid. Our (2) _ _ _ _ _ _ _ _ _ _, our (3) _ _ _ _ _ _ _ _ _ _ _ _

is still here, but now we have sites all over Spain, with about 500 employees. Many

of the offices are (4) _ _ _ _ - _ _ _ _: everyone works together, from managers to

(5) _ _ _ _ _ _ _ _ _ _ _ _ _ _ _ _ _ _, as well as people selling over the phone, and

people in technical (6) _ _ _ _ _ _ _ giving help to customers over the phone.

Recruitment is taken care of in Madrid, by the (7) _ _ _ _ _ _ _ _ _ _ _ _ _ _

_ _ _ _ _ _ _ _ _ _ or (8) _ _ _ .

Over to you

Think about the company you work for or one you would like to work for.
Where is its head office? How many sites does the company have? How many employees?
Is it better to have everyone on one site or to have different sites with different
activities? Do people have their own offices or are there open-plan offices?
Which type do you / would you prefer to work in?

7 The career ladder

A A job for life

Many people used to work for the same organization until they reached **retirement**: the age at which people **retire**, or end their working life. **Career paths** were clear: you could **work your way up the career ladder**, getting **promotion** to jobs that were more **senior**, with greater responsibility. You would probably not be **demoted**: moved to a less senior job.

To leave the company, you could **resign** or **hand in your notice**.

B A job for now

Modco has **downsized** and **delayered**. The number of management levels in the company hierarchy has been reduced from five to three, and many managers have lost their jobs. Modco has reorganized and **restructured** in order to become **flatter** (with fewer layers of management) and **leaner** (with fewer, more productive employees).

They did this to reduce costs, and increase **efficiency** and **profits**. Employees said the company used words like 'restructure' to make the situation sound positive and acceptable.

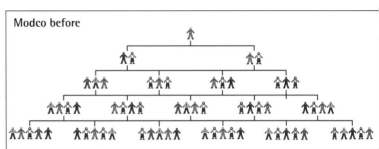

Modco before

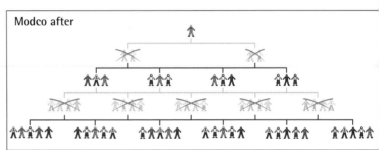

Modco after

C In-house staff or freelancers?

Modco has **outsourced** many jobs previously done by **in-house** personnel: outside companies clean the offices, transport goods and collect money from customers. This allows Modco to concentrate on its main business activities. Modco uses more **freelancers**, independent people who may work for several different companies, and they employ people for short periods on **temporary contracts**. Modco expects **flexibility**, with people moving to different jobs when necessary, but for many employees, this means **job insecurity**, the feeling that they may not be in their job for long. The way that they are doing their job is discussed at **performance reviews**: regular meetings with their manager.

Note: You say **freelancers** or **freelances**.

D Losing your job

If you do something wrong, you are ...

- dismissed
- fired
- sacked
- terminated

If you've done nothing wrong, you are ...

- laid off
- made redundant
- offered early retirement

Employees who are made redundant may get advice about finding another job, retraining, etc. This is called **outplacement** advice.

7.1 Complete the tables with forms of words from A, B and C opposite.
You may wish to refer to a dictionary.

Noun	Verb	Noun	Adjective
	retire	seniority	
demotion			freelance
lay-off		redundancy	
	dismiss		insecure
	terminate		flexible

7.2 Match the sentence beginnings (1–5) to the correct endings (a–e). The sentences all contain words from A and B opposite.

1 Career paths aren't what they used to be;
2 He worked his way up from
3 The new management have delayered the company,
4 We used to do printing in-house,
5 Workers are afraid their organizations will be downsized

a and they will be replaced by temporary workers.
b companies won't take care of us for life any more.
c but now we outsource it.
d factory worker to factory manager.
e reducing five management levels to three.

7.3 Carla used to work for an Italian magazine publishing company. She talks about how she lost her job. Choose the correct form of the words in brackets to complete the text.

Edizione Fenice is a big magazine publishing company, and a very nice company to work for. I was director of a magazine called *Casa e Giardino*.

Then, Fenice was bought by an international publishing group. We had to have regular performance (1) .... (review/reviews/reviewer) with one of the new managers. After a few months they started laying staff (2) .... (off/on/out). Our own journalists were put on temporary (3) .... (contracts/contractual/contracting) or replaced by (4) .... (freelancer/freelancers/freelanced).

Then they started (5) .... (laid/lying/laying) off more senior people like me. The new owners said they wanted to make the company (6) .... (flat/flatter/flatten) and (7) .... (lean/leant/leaner). So I was made (8) .... (redundant/redundancies/redundancy). They offered to help me to find another job with (9) .... (outplacement/outplaced/outplacing) advice, but I refused.

Over to you

If you work ...

Do you have performance reviews? What are the advantages and disadvantages? Has your organization been restructured? What aspects of the business does your company outsource?

If you don't work ...

Would you prefer a job for life or a more flexible career? Would you like regular performance reviews?

8 Problems at work

A Health and safety

Here are some **health and safety issues** for people at work.

a temperature

b passive smoking

c repetitive strain injury or RSI

d dangerous machinery

e hazardous substances

f fire hazards

All these things contribute to a **bad working environment**. The government sends officials called **health and safety inspectors** to make sure that factories and offices are safe places to work. They check what companies are doing about things like:

g heating and air-conditioning

h first aid

i fire precautions

B Bullying and harassment

If someone such as a manager **bullies** an employee, they use their position of power to hurt or threaten them, for example verbally. Someone who does this is a **bully**.

Sexual harassment is when an employee behaves sexually towards another in a way that they find unwelcome and unacceptable. The related verb is **harass**.

C Discrimination

If people are treated differently from others in an unfair way, they are **discriminated against**.

If a woman is unfairly treated just because she is a woman, she is a victim of **sex discrimination**. In many organizations, women complain about the **glass ceiling** that allows them to get to a particular level but no further.

If someone is treated unfairly because of their race, they are a victim of **racial discrimination** or **racism**. Offensive remarks about someone's race are **racist** and the person making them is **a racist**.

In the US, **affirmative action** is when help is given in education and employment to groups who were previously discriminated against. In Britain, affirmative action is known as **equal opportunities**.

Some companies have a **dignity at work policy** covering all the issues described in B and C.

8.1 Match the employees' complaints (1–6) to the health and safety issues (a–f) in A opposite.

1. *My doctor says there's something wrong with my lungs, but I've never smoked.* ......

2. *I do a lot of data entry, and I've started getting really bad pains in my wrists.* ......

3. *It's either too cold and we freeze, or too hot and we all fall asleep.* ......

4. *There's all this waste paper but there are no fire extinguishers in the building.* ......

5. *The containers are leaking – one day someone is going to get acid burns.* ......

6. *There are no safety guards on the machines; you could easily get your hand caught.* ......

8.2 Complete these headlines and articles with the correct form of words from B and C opposite. One expression is used twice.

1

OFFICE MANAGER ACCUSED OF ....

A court heard today how an office worker was almost driven to suicide by a bullying office manager. James Blenkinsop, 27, told how boss Nigel Kemp victimized him by shouting at him, criticizing his work in front of others, tearing up his work and telling him to do it again …

2

NATIONAL RESTAURANT CHAIN FACES .... CLAIMS

Four waitresses claim they were repeatedly .... by male bosses in a branch of a well-known national restaurant chain. All four waitresses said they were subjected to sexist remarks at the restaurant …

3

Japanese women break through ....

Naomi Tanaka, 23, last year started working on the Tokyo Stock Exchange as a trader. She complained about .... and said she did not want to be a 'counter lady' answering phones and serving tea at a Japanese bank. Instead she got a job as a trader at Paribas, a French firm …

4

SHOP MANAGERESS IN .... CASE

A clothing shop's half-Burmese manageress, 24-year-old Marion Brown, claims her boss continually made .... remarks, and sacked her from her £110-a-week job when she objected. She claims that the company that owns the shop has racially .... against her ...

5

.... ABOLISHED AT TEXAS LAW SCHOOL

A court made affirmative action at the University of Texas law school illegal last year, and supporters of .... say it has been 'a disaster'. Last year the law school admitted a class that was 5.9 per cent black and 6.3 per cent Hispanic. This year the black percentage stands at 0.7 and the Hispanic at 2.3 …

Over to you

What are the main health and safety issues in your job, or a job that you would like to do?

9 Managers, executives and directors

A ## Managers and executives: UK

Fun and Sun Holidays management organigram

| | non-executive directors | | chairman/chairwoman
chief executive/managing director | | | | |

**senior executives /
top executives /
executive directors**

| chief financial
officer/finance director | marketing
director | human resources
director | IT
director | research
director |

middle managers

| accounts department
manager | sales
manager | customer services
manager |

line managers (in travel agency branches)

All the **directors** together are the **board**. They meet in the **boardroom.**

Non-executive directors are not managers of the company; they are outsiders, often directors of other companies who have particular knowledge of the industry or of particular areas.

The marketing director is the **head of marketing**, the IT director is the **head of IT**, etc. These people **head** or **head up** their departments. Informally, the head of an activity, a department or an organization is its **boss.**

An **executive** or, informally, an **exec**, is usually a manager at quite a high level (for example, a **senior executive**). But 'executive' can be used in other contexts to suggest luxury, as in 'executive coach' and 'executive home', even for things that are not actually used by executives.

B ## Managers and executives: US

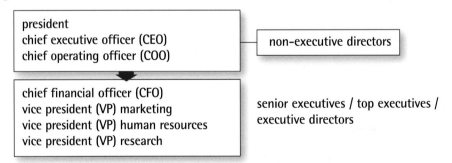

In the US, the top position may be that of chairman, chairwoman or **president**. This job is often combined with the position of **chief executive officer** or **CEO**. Some companies have a **chief operating officer** to take care of the day-to-day running of the company. The finance director may be called the **chief financial officer**.

In the US, senior managers in charge of particular areas are often called **vice presidents** (VPs).

9.1 Look at the managers listed in A opposite. Match each task (1–6) to the manager most likely to be responsible for doing it.

1 Meet with advertising agency to discuss new advertisements for the company's holidays.
2 Study possible new holiday destinations in detail.
3 See the research director to discuss new holiday destinations.
4 Contact newspapers to advertise new jobs.
5 Deal with complaints from customers.
6 Discuss sales figures with sales team.

9.2 Who's who on this company board? Look at B opposite and complete the diagram.

> My name's Montebello and I'm president and CEO. We have some excellent people on our board, including two who are not involved in the day-to-day running of the company: Gomi and Jones.

> My name's Smith and it's my job to look after the accounts and balance the books. I work closely with Chang and Roberts, as they tell me what their departments need for marketing and research, and I allocate them an annual budget.

> My name's Dawes and I head up personnel, on the same level in the company as Chang and Roberts.

_____ Montebello	Non-executive director _____	_____

_____	_____	_____	_____ Dawes

Over to you

If you work ...

Draw an organigram of your organization.

If you don't work ...

Who are the most famous bosses in your country? Which companies do they head?

10 Businesspeople and business leaders

A Businesspeople and entrepreneurs

A **businessman, businesswoman** or **businessperson** is someone who works in their own business or as a manager in an organization.

Note: The plural of businessperson is **businesspeople**. Businessperson and businesspeople can also be spelled as two words: **business person, business people**.

An **entrepreneur** is someone who starts or **founds** or **establishes** their own company. Someone who starts a company is its **founder**. An entrepreneur may found a series of companies or **start-ups**. **Entrepreneurial** is used in a positive way to describe the risk-taking people who do this, and their activities. Some entrepreneurs leave the companies they found, perhaps going on to found more companies. Others may stay to develop and **grow** their businesses.

Note: **Found** is a regular verb. Past tense and past participle: **founded**.
Establishment can also describe an action (e.g. the establishment of a successful business was his main aim in life).

! Some English speakers believe it is not correct to use **grow** as a transitive verb in this context.

B Leaders and leadership

A large company mainly owned by one person or family is a **business empire**. Successful businesspeople, especially heads of large organizations, are **business leaders** or, in journalistic terms, **captains of industry**.

There is a lot of discussion about whether people like this are born with **leadership skills**, or whether such skills can be learned.

C Magnates, moguls and tycoons

People in charge of big business empires may be referred to, especially by journalists, as **magnates**, **moguls** or **tycoons**. These words often occur in combinations such as these:

property

press

media press shipping oil	} magnate
movie media shipping	} mogul
property software	} tycoon

shipping

10.1 Use words from A and B opposite to complete this text.

The big place at the moment for (1) _ _ _ _ _ _ _ _ _ _ _ _ _ is, of course, the Internet. Take John Pace. 'After an engineering degree at Stanford and an MBA at Harvard, I worked for a while in a computer games company. But I always felt I was an (2) _ _ _ _ _ _ _ _ _ _ _ _ _ _ _ kind of guy. In 1997, I (3) _ _ _ _ _ _ _ an Internet site for cheap travel: flights, hotels, renting cars and so on. I obtained money for investment in the (4) _ _ _ _ _ - _ _ from friends.'

Now the site has 300,000 customers, and Pace is very rich, with a big apartment in Manhattan and a house in the Bahamas. 'I don't want to sell the company,' he says. 'I've had offers from some big companies, but I want to stay independent. I want to (5) _ _ _ _ the business and do things my way.

Unlike many entrepreneurs, I think I have the (6) _ _ _ _ _ _ _ _ _ _ skills to lead and inspire a large organization. I can see the day when I'm in charge of a large business (7) _ _ _ _ _ _ .'

10.2 Who are (or were) these famous businesspeople?
Use the expressions in C opposite to describe them.

a Randolph Hearst
(1863–1951)

b Masayoshi Son
(b. 1957)

c Rupert Murdoch
(b. 1931)

d Aristotle Onassis
(1906–1975)

e J. Paul Getty
(1892–1976)

f Donald Trump
(b. 1946)

Over to you

Who are your country's most famous entrepreneurs? What are they famous for?

In your opinion, are business leaders born or made?

11 Organizations 1

A Business and businesses

Business is the activity of producing, buying and selling goods and services. A **business, company, firm** or more formally, a **concern**, sells goods or services. Large companies considered together are referred to as **big business**.

A company may be called an **enterprise**, especially to emphasize its risk-taking nature.

Businesses vary in size, from the **self-employed** person working alone, through the **small** or **medium enterprise** (**SME**) to the large **multinational** with activities in several countries.

A large company, especially in the US, is a **corporation**. The adjective, **corporate**, is often used in these combinations:

- corporate culture
- corporate headquarters
- corporate image
- corporate ladder
- corporate logo
- corporate profits

B Commerce

Commerce is used to refer to business:
- in relation to other fields: 'literature, politics and commerce'.
- in relation to government departments that deal with business: the US **Department of Commerce**.
- in the names of organizations which help business: **chambers of commerce**.
- on the Internet: **electronic commerce** or **e-commerce**.

The adjective **commercial** describes money-making business activities:

- commercial airline
- commercial artist
- commercial television
- commercial disaster
- commercial land

 You can't say ~~a commerce~~.

C Enterprise

In 1970s Britain, there were **state-owned** or **government-owned** companies in many different industries such as car manufacturing and air travel. Some industries had been **nationalized** and were entirely state-owned, such as coal, electricity and telephone services. In the 1980s, the government believed that **nationalized companies** were **bureaucratic** and inefficient, and many of them were **privatized** and sold to investors.

Enterprise is used in a positive way to talk about business, emphasizing the use of money to take risks.

D Word combinations with 'enterprise'

free / private } enterprise		business activity owned by individuals, rather than the state
enterprise {	culture	an atmosphere which encourages people to make money through their own activities and not rely on the government
	economy	an economy where there is an enterprise culture
	zone	part of a country where business is encouraged because there are fewer laws, lower taxes, etc.

11.1 Correct the mistakes using words and expressions from A opposite.

1 Before we employ people, we like to put them in job situations to see how they do the work and fit into the corporate ladder.
2 The company has built a grand corporate logo as a permanent symbol of its power.
3 Our stylish new corporate culture shows our wish to be seen as a more international airline.
4 The economy is growing and corporate headquarters are rising.
5 The rules were introduced to protect women working in factories, but today they make it harder for women to climb the corporate image.
6 Companies hit by computer crime are not talking about it because they fear the publicity will harm their corporate profits.

11.2 Someone is talking about the word combinations in B opposite. Which are they referring to each time?

1 It carries passengers and goods, it's not military.
2 It's going to be used for offices and factories, not houses.
3 It receives no money from the state to make its programmes.
4 He does advertisements: you can't find his work in art galleries.
5 It was an artistic success, but unfortunately it lost a lot of money.

11.3 Use expressions from D opposite to complete this text.

Margaret Thatcher often talked about the benefits of (1) ....
or (2) .... She said that her achievement was to establish an
(3) .... in Britain, an economy where people were
encouraged to start their own companies and where it was acceptable to get rich through
business: an (4) ....

In some areas, the government reduced the number of laws and regulations
to encourage businesses to move there. Businesses were encouraged to set up in the
London Docklands, for example. The Docklands were an (5) ....
....

Over to you

Is the public sector in your country very big? Do people who work in it have good working conditions compared to those in the private sector?

In your country, which of these industries are in the public sector, and which are in the private sector? Which have been privatized?

- bus transport
- rail transport
- electricity supply
- telephone services
- postal services
- water supply

12 Organizations 2

A Self-employed people and partnerships

I'm a **freelance** graphic designer, a **freelancer**. That means I work for myself – I'm **self-employed**. To use the official term, I'm a **sole trader**.

Note: You usually describe people such as designers and journalists as **freelancers**, and people such as builders and plumbers as **self-employed**. (See Unit 7)

> **Sole owner** and **sole proprietor** are also used both in BrE and AmE. **Sole trader** is not used in the US.

We have set up our own architecture **partnership**. There are no shareholders in the organization apart from us, the partners. A lot of professional people like lawyers, accountants and so on, work in partnerships.

B Limited liability

> I'm the managing director and main shareholder of a small electronics company in Scotland called Advanced Components **Ltd**. 'Ltd' means **limited company**. The other shareholders and I have **limited liability**: we do not have to use our personal property, such as a house or car, to pay the company's debts.

> I'm the chief executive of a British company called Megaco **PLC**. 'PLC' means **public limited company**, so anybody can buy and sell shares in Megaco on the stock market. (See Unit 36)

> I'm CEO of Bigbucks **Inc**. 'Inc' stands for **Incorporated**. This shows that we are a **corporation**, a term used especially in the US for companies with limited liability.

C Mutuals

Some companies, like certain **life insurance companies**, are **mutuals**. When you buy insurance with the company you become a **member**. Profits are theoretically owned by the members, so there are no shareholders.

In Britain, another kind of mutual is **building societies**, which lend money to people who want to buy a house. But a lot of building societies have **demutualized**: they have become public limited companies with shareholders. This process is **demutualization**.

D Non-profit organizations

Organizations with 'social' aims such as helping those who are sick or poor, or encouraging artistic activity, are **non-profit organizations** (BrE) or **not-for-profit organizations** (AmE). They are also called **charities**, and form the **voluntary sector**, as they rely heavily on **volunteers** (unpaid workers). They are usually managed by paid professionals, and they put a lot of effort into **fund-raising**, getting people to **donate** money to the organization in the form of **donations**.

12.1 Look at the words in A and B opposite. What type of organization is each of these?

1 A group of engineers who work together to provide consultancy and design services. There are no outside shareholders.
2 A large British engineering company with 30,000 employees. Its shares are bought and sold on the stock market.
3 An American engineering company with outside shareholders.
4 An engineer who works by herself providing consultancy. She works from home and visits clients in their offices.
5 An independent British engineering company with 20 employees. It was founded by three engineers, who are shareholders and directors of the company. There are five other shareholders who do not work for the company.

12.2 Complete this newspaper article with the correct form of the words from C opposite. One expression is used twice.

ANGRY SCENES AS MEMBERS REJECT (1) ....

There were angry scenes at the Suffolk (2) ....'s annual meeting as the society's (3) .... rejected by two to one a recommendation from its board that the society be (4) .... Members had travelled from all over the country to attend the meeting in London. The Suffolk's chief executive, Mr Andrew Davies, said 'This is a sad day for the Suffolk. We need to (5) .... to bring the society forward into the 21st century. Our own resources are not enough and we need capital from outside shareholders.'

Gwen Armstrong, who has saved with the Suffolk for 32 years said, 'Keeping (6) .... status is a great victory. Profits should stay with us, and not go to outside shareholders.' ∎

12.3 Match the sentence beginnings (1–5) to the correct endings (a–e).
The sentences all contain expressions from D opposite.

1 British companies donate around £500 million a year to charities
2 She organized fund-raising
3 Voluntary sector employees earn five to ten per cent
4 Non-profit organizations are not to be confused
5 Research shows that volunteers give the best service

a with loss-making companies!
b in cash and, increasingly, as goods, services and time.
c parties for the charity.
d when they are helping people in their own social class.
e less than they would in the private sector.

Over to you

Is self-employment common in your country? Does the government encourage it?

Name some mutual companies. What sort of reputation do they have?

Are charities important? Which are the most active in your country?

13 Manufacturing and services

A Industry

Industry (uncountable) is the production of materials and goods. The related adjective is **industrial**. **An industry** (countable) is a particular type of business activity, not necessarily production.

B Manufacturing ...

Here are some of the **manufacturing industries** that make up the **manufacturing sector**:

aerospace	planes and space vehicles
cars (BrE) **automobiles** (AmE)	cars
computer hardware	computers, printers, etc.
construction	buildings
defence (BrE) **defense** (AmE)	arms, weapons
food processing	canned, frozen foods, etc.
household goods	washing machines, refrigerators, etc.
pharmaceuticals	medicines
steel	a stronger, more useful metal than iron
textiles	cloth and clothes

... and services

Here are some of the **services** or **service industries** that make up the **service sector**:

catering	restaurants, bars, etc.
computer software	programs for computers
financial services	banking, insurance, etc.
healthcare	medical care
leisure	sport, theme parks, etc.
media	books, newspapers, film, television
property (BrE) **real estate** (AmE)	buying, selling and managing buildings
retail	shops
telecommunications	phone, Internet services
tourism	travel and holidays

Note: You use all these words in front of 'industry' to talk about particular industries, but you usually drop the 's' from 'cars', 'automobiles', 'pharmaceuticals' and 'textiles': 'the automobile industry'.

C Countries and their industries

Here is how industry has developed in South Korea:

1950s and 60s

In 1950, South Korea was a poor country, with most people living and working on the land. The government decided to **industrialize**, and the new **emerging industries** were textiles, and **heavy industries** like steel and shipbuilding.

1970s

Then South Korea turned more and more to **light industries** like electronics, making electrical goods such as televisions cheaply. It also started producing cars.

1980s and 90s

South Korea moved into specialized electronics in the 80s. This was the one of the **growth industries** of the 1990s: making specialized parts for computers and telecommunications equipment.

13.1 Companies in particular industries need to avoid particular problems. Match each problem to one of the industries in B opposite.

1 Buying a new building and being unable to find people to rent it.
2 Causing public anger by building mobile phone masts in beautiful countryside.
3 Making vehicles whose tyres burst at high speed.
4 Holidaymakers arriving to find that their hotel is not finished.
5 Lending to someone who cannot repay the loan.
6 Selling weapons to governments that people do not approve of.
7 Buying players who do not score goals.
8 Making drugs that poor countries cannot afford.
9 Rejecting a book that is then brought out by another publisher and sells 30 million copies.
10 Removing the wrong leg in an operation.

13.2 Use words from A, B and C opposite to complete the crossword.

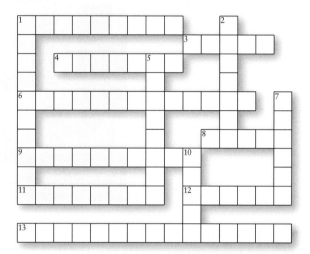

Across
1 Plane and rocket industry. (9)
3 Metal industry. (5)
4 Any industry that doesn't sell goods. (7)
6 Making things. (13)
8 Television, music, the Internet. (5)
9 Related to industry or industries. (10)
11 Describing a new industry. (8)
12 Describing an industry that is getting bigger. (6)
13 Making drugs. (15)

Down
1 Making cars in the US: the .... industry. (10)
2 Making arms (BrE). (7)
5 Serving food and drink, rather than making them. (8)
7 Keeping people well: .... care. (6)
10 Making televisions rather than steel: .... industry. (5)

Over to you

Is your organization, or one you would like to work for, in manufacturing or services or a combination of both?

Where are industries in your country based? Are companies in different industries grouped in different areas?

14 The development process

A Market research

The **original concept** is the basic idea for something.

In designing products and services, **market research** – finding out what people want – is of course very important. This may involve **questionnaires** or **surveys**, with questions about what people buy and why, perhaps with interviews in the street or by telephone.

There may be **consumer panels** and **focus groups**, where ordinary people meet to discuss product ideas informally.

Perhaps the researchers will make **sales forecasts**, estimates of how many products will be sold.

See Unit 21 for more on marketing.

B Development and launch

In software, developers often produce a final test version, the **beta version**, where users are asked to point out **bugs** (problems) before the software is finalized.

Car **designers** use **CADCAM (computer-assisted design / computer-assisted manufacturing)** to help develop and make products and test different **prototypes**.

Researchers in **laboratories** may take years to develop new drugs, **testing** or **trialling** them in **trials** to show not only that they are **effective**, but also that they are **safe**. Drugs need to be made on an **industrial scale** before they can be sold.

Rollout is the process of making a product available, perhaps in particular places, to test reaction.

Product launch is the moment when the product is officially made available for sale. This is the 'big moment'.

If a **design defect** or **design fault** is found in a product after it has been launched, the company may have to **recall** it, asking those who have bought it to return it, perhaps so that the defect can be corrected.

14.1 Three people are talking about their work in product development. Correct the mistakes in italics, using expressions from A and B opposite.

1

(a) *Market researches showed* there was a real need for this service, but before offering it, we had to test it in a (b) *beta copy* with small groups of users over several months to eliminate all the bugs. Even so, (c) *after lunch*, some users said they could get into other people's accounts!

2

The more you eat, the thinner you get, and (d) *the focal groups* said they liked the taste, but first we had to prove to the authorities that it was (e) *secure*. Another problem was making it on an (f) *industrial level*: at first we could only make it in small quantities in the laboratory, but making it in bigger quantities was impossible.

3

At our research centre in Toulouse in France, the (g) *designators* develop the prototypes. People think that my job is dangerous, but there is so much (h) *tasting* on computer first, that all the danger has been eliminated by the time we use the product. (i) *CADCAR* means that the process of design and manufacture is much quicker than before.

14.2 Complete this talk by a marketing specialist using words from A and B opposite.

A few years ago a famous car company launched a new car, based on a completely new (1) .... They'd done years of technical research and (2) .... research with focus (3) .... and (4) .... panels and analysis of responses to questionnaires and (5) .... Then came the (6) .... Sales of the car were very good until a Swedish newspaper reported the results of its 'elk test'. They found that the car had a tendency to tip over if you turned quickly to avoid an elk. This was due to a (7) .... fault in the car, so they had to (8) .... all the cars they'd sold in order to correct it.

Over to you

What sort of market research does your company, or one you would like to work for, do? Have you ever taken part in market research as a consumer?

15 Innovation and invention

A Innovation and invention

Verb	Noun: concept (uncountable)	Noun: thing (countable)	Noun: person
design: to make plans or drawings for how something is to be made	design	a design	a designer
develop: to make a new idea successful, for example by making or improvinga product	development	a development	a developer
innovate: to think of new ideas, methods, products, etc.	innovation	an innovation	an innovator
invent: to design and make something for the first time	invention	an invention	an inventor
–	**technology**: the practical or industrial use of scientific discoveries	a technology	a technologist

countable = you can say *a/an*; uncountable = you can't say *a/an*

B Research and technology

Hi, I'm Ray and I'm head of **product development** at Lightning Technologies. Lightning makes semiconductors, the components at the heart of every computer. I'm in charge of **research and development (R&D)** at our **research centre** just outside Boston. Our **laboratories** are some of the most **innovative** in the computer industry, and we have made many new discoveries and **breakthroughs**.

I love **technology**, using scientific **knowledge** for practical purposes. The **technology** of semiconductors is fascinating. We are at the **cutting edge** or **leading edge** of semiconductor technology: none of our competitors has better products than us. Everything we do is **state-of-the-art**, using the most advanced techniques available.

Of course, the **hi-tech** products of today become the **low-tech** products of tomorrow. Products that are no longer up-to-date because they use old technology are **obsolete**. It's my job to make sure that Lightning's products never get into that situation.

> BrE: research centre
> AmE: research center

C Patents and intellectual property

Information or knowledge that belongs to an individual or company is **proprietary**. A product developed using such information may be protected in law by **patents** so that others cannot copy its design.

	Noun	Verb
BrE:	a licence	to license
AmE:	a license	to license

Other companies may pay to use the design **under licence** in their own products. These payments are **royalties**.

In publishing, if a text, picture, etc. is **copyright**, it cannot be used by others without permission. Payments to the author from the publisher are **royalties**.

The area of law relating to patents and copyright is **intellectual property**.

15.1 Choose the correct forms to complete these sentences containing words from A opposite.

1 White came up with (a design/design) that combined lightness and warmth.
2 There's an exhibition on architecture and (the design/design) at the Museum of Modern Art.
3 McGrew is vice president of (a development/development) and product planning.
4 The FDA has approved (a development/development) for treating tooth disease, a new laser machine.
5 Electric light was (an invention/invention) which enabled people to stay up later.
6 Sometimes (an invention/invention) is so obvious that it is hard to believe nobody thought of it before.
7 Channel Four has always encouraged experimentation and (an innovation/innovation) in its films.
8 He discovered (an innovation/innovation) that has enabled him to build guitars more efficiently.

15.2 Complete this presentation using words from B opposite. Put the words in brackets into their correct form.

Hi, I'm Raj (1) .... I'm head (2) .... product (3 develop) .... at
(4) .... Indian Rice Research Centre. I'm in charge of research (5) ....
development (6) .... our (7 researching) .... centre in Delhi. Our
(8 laboratory) .... are (9) .... of the most (10 innovation) ....
(11) .... agriculture. We have recently (12) .... some big
(13 breakthrough) .... in increasing rice production.

I love (14 technological) .... , using scientific knowledge (15) .... improve
people's lives. (16) .... technology (17) .... rice development (18) ....
a good example (19) .... this.

We are at the (20) .... edge of rice-growing techniques. Everything we do
(21) .... state-of-the-art, using the most advanced biological (22 know) ....
available.

15.3 Match the expressions (1–6) from C opposite with their meanings (a–f).

1 copyright infringement
2 intellectual property
3 patent application
4 proprietary information
5 royalty payment
6 licensing agreement

a a payment to the owner of a design, or to an author
b an arrangement between the owner of a design and someone else, allowing them to use the design for money
c when someone uses another's text, pictures, etc. without permission
d when an inventor asks the authorities to officially recognize an invention as his/her property
e designs, ideas, etc. that belong to someone
f the law relating to designs, ideas, etc. that belong to someone

Over to you

For you, which is the most important invention of the last 100 years?
Which one do you wish had not been invented?

16 Making things

A Products

A **product** can be:

- something natural.
- something made to be sold.
- a service.

Produce refers to agricultural products such as crops or fruit.
For example, you can buy fresh produce at a farmers' market

Something that is made is **produced** or **manufactured**.

A country or company that produces something is a **producer** of it.

A company that manufactures something is a **maker** or **manufacturer** of **manufactured goods**.

B Mass production

'I'm Steve and I'm head of car production at a **manufacturing plant**. 'Plant' sounds more modern than **factory** or **works**. On the **assembly line** we **mass-produce** cars. The plant is highly **automated**: we use a lot of machinery. These machines are expensive to buy but very **cost-effective** – we don't have to pay them wages! We use **industrial robots**. These robots are part of the **CADCAM** system of computer-assisted design and manufacturing.'

> BrE: labour-intensive
> AmE: labor-intensive

'My name's Luke. I have a little **workshop** where I produce furniture ordered by individual customers. We don't use machinery: the furniture is **hand-made**. Producing furniture like this is a **craft industry**. It's very **labour-intensive**: it takes a lot of work to produce each piece. Many people dislike the furniture that big companies **churn out** in large numbers on their **production lines**, so we have a lot of customers.'

CADCAM system

Craft industry

C Capacity and output

Output is the number or type of things that a plant, company, industry or country produces. **Productivity** is a measure of how much is produced in relation to the number of employees. High output per employee = high productivity.

The maximum amount that a particular plant, company or industry can produce is its **capacity**. If it is producing this amount, it is **working at full capacity**. If it is producing more than what is needed, there is **overproduction** or:

- excess capacity
- overcapacity
- spare capacity
- surplus capacity

These expressions can also be used in service industries.

If far too many things are produced, there is a **glut** of these things. If not enough goods are being produced, there is a **shortage**.

16.1 Complete this table with words from A opposite.

Verb	Noun: person/organization	Noun: process	Noun: thing
make	maker	×	×
		manufacturing	
produce: non-food		production	
produce: food		production	

16.2 Rearrange these lines to make a text containing words from B and C opposite.

1 work. Of course, we still have a lot of assembly
2 plant producing TVs in Singapore. We have two production
3 My name's George Chen, and I'm director of a manufacturing
4 lines working 24 hours a day. We use CAD
5 line workers, so it's still quite labour-
6 intensive. But with the help of computer-
7 CAM, and robots do some assembly
8 assisted design and automation, productivity is increasing.

16.3 Match the headlines (1–7) to the extracts they relate to (a–g).

1 **FOOD SHORTAGES HIT EASTERN AFRICA**

2 **AIRLINE REPORTS BIG PRODUCTIVITY RISE**

3 **TOO MUCH BUILDING LEADS TO GLUT OF OFFICE SPACE**

4 **LOCAL PLANT AT FULL CAPACITY**

5 **FALL IN STUDENT NUMBERS LEADS TO EDUCATION OVERCAPACITY**

6 **OIL OVERPRODUCTION LEADS TO PRICE FALL**

7 **NATIONAL OUTPUT AT ALL-TIME HIGH**

a ... Overall production in the country rose by five per cent last year ...
b ... Rainfall has been below average in this part of Africa for the past five years. Not enough food has been grown ...
c ... Too much oil has been produced recently in relation to world demand ...
d ... There have never been so few people aged between 17 and 21 since 1950. The result: too many places at private colleges and universities ...
e ... The plant's capacity is 3,000 computers a week, and it's producing 3,000 ...
f ... Northern is running more flights with fewer pilots and staff. That was the message from Northern's CEO Frank Delaney to shareholders yesterday ...
g ... There has been too much building in the city centre, and now there is a lot of office space standing empty ...

Over to you

Are hand-made goods necessarily better than factory-made ones?
What about cars, clothes, computers and shoes?

17 Materials and suppliers

A Inputs

Dryden makes vacuum cleaners. It takes **raw materials** like steel and plastic and makes some of the **components** or **parts** used in its products. Other components are made by other companies.

Materials and parts are just some of the inputs. The others are **labour** (workers and managers) and **capital** (money). **Knowledge** is also important because Dryden is a leader in vacuum technology.

Vacuum cleaners that are being made are **work-in-progress**. At any one time, Dryden has **goods** worth millions of dollars in its factories and warehouses: the products that have been made – its **finished goods** – and materials and components.

Quantities of raw materials, components, work-in-progress and finished goods in a particular place are **stocks**.

Note: **Goods** is rarely used in the singular.

Work-in-progress

> BrE: **work-in-progress**; AmE: **work-in-process**
> BrE: **stocks**; AmE: **inventories**

B Suppliers and outsourcing

Dryden receives materials and components from about 20 companies, its **suppliers** or **partners**.

The company is doing more **subcontracting**: using **outside suppliers** to provide components and services. In other words, it is **outsourcing** more, using outside suppliers for goods or services that were previously supplied **in-house**: within the company.

C Just-in-time

Of course, it costs money to keep components and goods **in stock**: stocks have to be **financed** (paid for), **stored** (perhaps in special buildings: **warehouses**) and handled (moved from one place to another). So Dryden is asking its suppliers to provide components **just-in-time**, as and when they are needed.

This is part of **lean production** or **lean manufacturing**, making things efficiently: doing things as quickly and cheaply as possible, without waste.

A warehouse

17.1 Use words from A opposite to label the diagram.

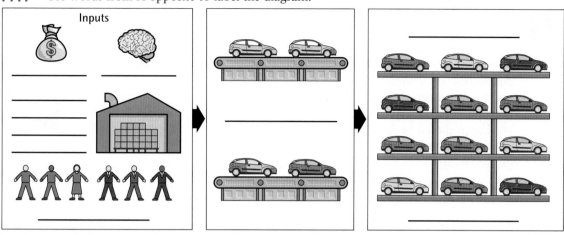

17.2 Match the sentence beginnings (1–4) with the correct endings (a–d).
The sentences all contain words from B opposite.

1 Computer manufacturer XL is cutting back on in-

a contractors' maintenance work is worrying train operating companies.

2 The poor standard of some sub

b suppliers are causing delays in production, the Azco group claims.

3 Retail giant Sharks Ltd have decided to out

c house production work in a bid to reduce costs and increase efficiency.

4 Late deliveries from outside

d source canteen and cleaning services, to focus better on its buying and selling activities.

17.3 Replace the words in speech bubbles with the correct forms of words from C opposite.

1 Let's get the materials in ⟨ *only when we need them* ⟩ to keep costs down.

2 It's difficult to find the right ⟨ *special buildings* ⟩ to put our finished goods in.

3 You'll have to decide well in advance how ⟨ *to pay* ⟩ for all this.

4 It's very important that we ⟨ *keep* ⟩ these components at the right temperature.

5 There must be a ⟨ *quicker and cheaper* ⟩ method than this!

6 They want to introduce a system of ⟨ *making things efficiently.* ⟩

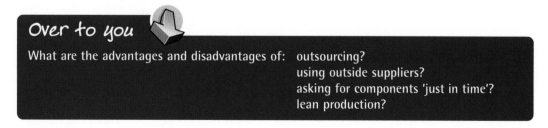

Over to you

What are the advantages and disadvantages of: outsourcing?
using outside suppliers?
asking for components 'just in time'?
lean production?

18 Business philosophies

A Total quality management

Tom Dryden, of Dryden Vacuum Cleaners, believes in **quality**: 'The **specifications** or **specs** of a product are exact instructions about its design, including its **dimensions** (size), how it is to be made, the materials to be used, etc. The objective of **quality control** is **conformity** to **specifications**, the idea that the product should be made exactly as it was intended, with **zero defects**: no faults at all. Things should be done **right first time** so we don't have to correct mistakes later in a process of **reworking**. We do **spot checks** every few minutes during production to ensure everything is going well.

We have a system of **total quality management** (**TQM**), including **quality circles**: groups of employees who meet regularly to suggest improvements.'

B Continuous improvement

Ray, at Lightning Technologies: 'We are always making small improvements or **enhancements**; this is **continuous improvement**. We refer to it by its Japanese name: **kaizen**.'

Silvia Chavez, Aerolíneas Latinas: 'We use continuous improvement in our service industry. We look carefully at the overall customer experience. In retailing, they use **mystery shoppers**, who pretend to be shoppers to check service in shops. We use "mystery travellers" to report on the standard of service before, during and after the flight.'

C Benchmarking

Jim, production manager at an electricity power station in the UK: 'We use a system called **benchmarking** to compare our **performance** to other power stations. We've recently been to the US to see how the best power stations operate – **best practice** – and try to copy it. We've managed to halve the number of workers, and increase productivity.'

D Business process re-engineering

Susanna, head of personal banking at an international bank: '**Business process re-engineering**, or **BPR**, applies in service industries as well as in manufacturing. We didn't want to change existing things in small ways. We completely redesigned all our processes in management, administration and customer service. We eliminated three levels of management and installed a completely new computer system. The gains in productivity have been very good.'

18.1 Complete the crossword, using words from A opposite.

Across
3 See 6 down.
4,5 down Right .... (5,4)
8 Could be length, height or width. (9)
11 Total quality .... (10)
12,10 Making sure things are alright. (4,6)

Down
1 What the designer decides. (13)
2 Doing it again when you shouldn't have to. (9)
5 See 4 across.
6,3 across No mistakes at all. (4,7)
7 A quality .... meets to suggest improvements. (6)
9 Short form of 1 down in plural. (5)

18.2 Which expression from B, C or D opposite describes each of these situations? One of the expressions is used twice.

1 A police service reduces the number of forms to fill in when a crime is reported, first from fifteen to twelve, then to ten, then to seven, then to three.
2 A travel company closes all its high street shops, lays off middle managers and half of its sales assistants and retrains the others to sell on the phone. It also starts an Internet service.
3 A telephone company looks at other telephone companies to see which one issues bills with fewest mistakes to customers. It then copies this company's methods to reduce the mistakes in its own bills.
4 Most parcel delivery companies deliver 70 per cent of parcels by 10 am the next day, but one company has an advanced computer system that enables it to achieve an 80 per cent delivery rate.
5 An Internet banking service starts by allowing customers to see how much money they have in their accounts, and the latest transactions in the order they took place. Six months later customers can view the transactions in different orders. Three months later, they can make payments using the Internet service, which they couldn't do before.

Over to you

Do you try to continuously improve your own work? If so, in what ways?

In what ways does your company or the place where you study improve its efficiency? What should it be doing?

19 Buyers, sellers and the market

A Customers and clients

Company	Products/services	Customer / client base
Autocomp	products: car components	**customer base**: car companies
Best Travel	services: package holidays	**customer base**: general public
Digby and Charles	professional services: architecture	**client base** or **clientele**: companies, government organizations and the public
Digitco	products: cheap computers	**customer base**: general public

People who buy 'everyday' services such as train travel or telephone services are called **customers**. You can also talk about the **users** or **end-users** of a product or service, who may not be the people who actually buy it. For example, when a company buys computers for its staff to use, the staff are the end-users.

People who buy products or services for their own use are **consumers**, especially when considered as members of large groups of people buying things in advanced economies.

B Buyers and sellers

A person or organization that buys something is a **buyer** or **purchaser**. These words also describe someone in a company who is responsible for buying goods that the company uses or sells. These people are also **buying managers** or **purchasing managers**.

A person or organization that sells something is a **seller**. In some contexts, for example selling property, they are referred to as the **vendor**. People selling things in the street are **street vendors**.

Street vendors

C The market

The market, the free market and **market economy** describe an economic system where prices, jobs, wages, etc. are not controlled by the government, but depend on what people want to buy and how much they are willing to pay.

D Word combinations with 'market'

market	**forces** **pressures**	the way a market economy makes sellers produce what people want, at prices they are willing to pay
	place	producers and buyers in a particular market economy, and the way they behave
	prices	prices that people are willing to pay, rather than ones fixed by a government
	reforms	changes a government makes to an economy, so that it becomes more like a market economy

Note: **Marketplace** is written as a single word.

19.1 Find expressions in A and B opposite with the following meanings.

1 Someone who buys food in a supermarket. (3 expressions)
2 All the people who buy food from a particular supermarket chain, from the point of view of the chain.
3 Someone who buys the services of a private detective agency.
4 All the people who buy the services of a private detective agency, seen as a group. (2 expressions)
5 Someone who sells goods or services.
6 Someone selling a house. (2 expressions)
7 Someone buying a house. (2 expressions)
8 Someone who sells hamburgers to tourists outside the Tower of London.
9 Someone whose job is buying tyres for a car company. (4 expressions)
10 Someone who uses a computer, even if they have not bought it themself, but their company has. (2 expressions)

19.2 Complete the TV reporter's commentary with expressions from C and D opposite.

In China, all economic activity used to be controlled by the state. Prices were fixed by the government, not by buyers and sellers in the market (1) .... But in the last 20 years there has been a series of market (2) .... that have allowed people to go into business and start their own companies. Market (3) .... are determined by what buyers are willing to pay, rather than by the state. There are still state-owned companies that lose a lot of money. Until recently, they have been protected from market (4) .... , but market (5) .... will eventually mean that they close down. Of course, the market (6) .... has its losers: those without work, and victims of crime, which used to be very rare.

Over to you

What goods or services does your company, or one you would like to work for, sell?
Does it sell to the public, or to other companies?

20 Markets and competitors

Companies and markets

You can talk about the people or organizations who buy particular goods or services as the **market** for them, as in the 'car market', 'the market for financial services', etc. Buyers and sellers of particular goods or services in a place, or those that might buy them, form a **market**.

If a company:

enters penetrates		it starts selling there for the first time.
abandons gets out of leaves		it stops selling there.
dominates	a market	it is the most important company selling there.
corners monopolizes		it is the only company selling there.
drives another company out of		it makes the other company leave the market, perhaps because it can no longer compete.

More word combinations with 'market'

'Market' is often used in these combinations:

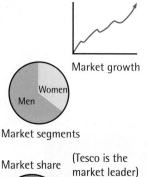

Market growth

Market segments

Market share

(Tesco is the market leader)
- Safeway
- Sainsbury's
- Waitrose
- Asda
- other

market	growth	In the late 1990s, Internet use was doubling every 100 days. **Market growth** was incredible.
	segment	Women are a particularly interesting target for the Volvo V70. They are an important **market segment** for Volvo.
	segmentation	The Softco software company divides the software market into large companies, small companies, home office users, and leisure users. This is its **market segmentation**.
	share	Among UK supermarkets, Tesco sells more than any of the other chains. It has the highest **market share**.
	leader	Tesco is the **market leader** among UK supermarkets as it sells more than any of the other chains.

Competitors and competition

Companies or products in the same market are **competitors** or **rivals**. Competitors **compete** with each other to sell more, be more successful, etc.

The most important companies in a particular market are often referred to as **key players**.

Competition describes the activity of trying to sell more and be more successful. When competition is strong, you can say that it is **intense, stiff, fierce** or **tough**. If not, it may be described as **low-key**.

The competition refers to all the products, businesses, etc. competing in a particular situation, seen as a group.

20.1 Use the correct form of the words in brackets to complete the sentences.

1 European films do not export well: European movies barely .... (abandon/corner/penetrate) the US market.

2 In the 1970s, Kodak .... (corner/enter/leave) the instant photography market, until then .... (abandon/dominate/penetrate) by Polaroid.

3 The Hunt brothers tried to fix silver prices and to .... (corner/enter/leave) the silver market, ... (enter/drive out/monopolize) all competitors.

4 In the 1940s, MGM .... (abandon/get out of/monopolize) the market on film musicals. But by the late 1950s, Warner Bros had also started buying film rights to musicals.

20.2 Replace the underlined expressions with expressions from B opposite. You may need to add a verb in the correct form.

I'm Kalil and I'm marketing manager for CrazyCola in a country called Newmarket. In this market, we (1) <u>sell more than any other cola</u>. In fact, we (2) <u>have 55 per cent of the market</u>. (3) <u>Sales are increasing at</u> seven to eight per cent per year. There are two main (4) <u>groups of users</u>: those who drink it in cafés, bars and restaurants, and those who buy it to drink at home. Of course, many users belong to both groups, but this is our (5) <u>way of dividing our consumers</u>.

20.3 Read this description of a language training market. Answer the questions.

In Paris, 500 organizations offer language training to companies. However, 90 per cent of sales are made by the top five language training organizations. The market is not growing in size overall. Organization A has 35 per cent of the market, and faces stiff competition from B, which has about 25 per cent of the market, and from C, D and E, who each have 10 per cent, but who are trying to grow by charging less for their courses.

1 How many competitors are there in this market?
2 Is competition in the market strong?
3 Who is the market leader?
4 Who are the two key players?
5 Who mainly makes up the competition, from the market leader's point of view?
6 If one competitor increases its market share, can the others keep their market share at the same level?

Over to you

Answer the questions in 20.3 about a market that you know, for example the market that your company, or a company you would like to work for, is in.

21 Marketing and market orientation

A Marketing

Marketing is the process of planning, designing, pricing, promoting and distributing ideas, goods and services, in order to satisfy **customer needs**, so as to make a profit.

Companies point out how the special characteristics or **features** of their products and services possess particular **benefits** that satisfy the needs of the people who buy them.

Non-profit organizations have other, social, goals, such as persuading people not to smoke, or to give money to people in poor countries, but these organizations also use the techniques of marketing.

In some places, even organizations such as government departments are starting to talk about, or at least think about their activities in terms of the **marketing concept**.

B The four Ps

The four Ps are

product: deciding what to sell

price: deciding what prices to charge

place: deciding how it will be distributed and where people will buy it

promotion: deciding how the product will be supported with advertising, special activities, etc.

A fifth P which is sometimes added is **packaging**: all the materials used to protect and present a product before it is sold.

The four Ps are a useful summary of the **marketing mix**, the activities that you have to combine successfully in order to sell. The next four units look at these activities in detail.

Promotion

To market a product is to make a plan based on this combination and put it into action. A **marketer** or **marketeer** is someone who works in this area.

(**Marketer** can also be used to describe an organization that sells particular goods or services.)

C Market orientation

Marketers often talk about **market orientation**: the fact that everything they do is designed to meet the needs of the market. They may describe themselves as **market-driven**, **market-led** or **market-oriented**.

21.1 Look at A and B opposite. Read the article and answer the questions.

> ## Most people and many managers do not understand the role of marketing in modern business.
>
> Marketing is two things. First, it is a strategy and set of techniques to sell an organization's products or services. This involves choosing target customers and designing a persuasive marketing mix to get them to buy. The mix may include a range of brands, tempting prices, convenient sales outlets and a battery of advertising and promotions. This concept of marketing as selling and persuasion is by far the most popular idea among both managers and the public.
>
> The second, and by far more important concept of marketing, focuses on improving the reality of what is on offer. It is based on understanding customers' needs and developing new solutions which are better than those currently available. Doing this is not a marketing department problem, but one which involves the whole organization.
>
> For example, for Rover to beat Mercedes for the consumer's choice involves engineering new models, developing lean manufacturing processes, and restructuring its dealer network.
>
> Creating company-wide focus on the customer requires the continual acquisition of new skills and technology. Marketing is rarely effective as a business function. As the chief executive of Hewlett Packard put it: 'Marketing is too important to leave to the marketing department.' Such companies understand that everybody's task is marketing. This concept of marketing offering real customer value is what business is all about.

1 Which of the four Ps are mentioned here?
2 Does the author think the four Ps are a complete definition of marketing?
3 Does the author think that marketing is only for marketers?

21.2 Match the sentence beginnings (1–5) with the correct endings (a–e). The sentences all contain expressions from C opposite.

1 Farms are now more market-oriented
2 Since the 1980s, Britain has had a much more market-led
3 Many market-led growth businesses,
4 Lack of investment and market orientation
5 American TV is a market-driven industry,

a such as Microsoft and Sony, are in several markets at once.
b and the audience decides the direction it takes.
c led to falling sales and profits.
d and less dependent on government money.
e approach to economics.

Over to you

Can a poor product be made successful by clever marketing techniques?
Can you think of any examples?

22 Products and brands

A Word combinations with 'product'

product	catalogue (BrE) catalog (AmE) mix portfolio	a company's products, as a group
	line range	a company's products of a particular type
	lifecycle	the stages in the life of a product, and the number of people who buy it at each stage
	positioning	how a company would like a product to be seen in relation to its other products, or to competing products
	placement	when a company pays for its products to be seen in films and TV programmes

See Units 15 and 16 for verbs used to talk about products.

B Goods

Goods can refer to the materials and components used to make products, or the products that are made.

Here are some examples of these different types of goods:

Consumer goods that last a long time, such as cars and washing machines, are **consumer durables**. Consumer goods such as food products that sell quickly are **fast-moving consumer goods**, or **FMCG**.

Raw materials

Finished goods

C Brands and branding

A **brand** is a name a company gives to its products so they can be easily recognized. This may be the name of the company itself: the **make** of the product. For products like cars, you refer to the make and **model**, the particular type of car, for example, the Ford (make) Ka (model).

Brand awareness or **brand recognition** is how much people recognize a brand. The ideas people have about a brand is its **brand image**. Many companies have a **brand manager**.

Branding is creating brands and keeping them in customer's minds through advertising, packaging, etc. A brand should have a clear **brand identity** so that people think of it in a particular way in relation to other brands.

A product with the retailer's own name on it is an **own-brand product** (BrE) or **own-label product** (AmE).

Products that are not **branded**, those that do not have a **brand name**, are **generic products** or **generics**.

22.1 Match the sentence beginnings (1–7) with the correct endings (a–g). The sentences all contain expressions from A opposite.

1 Banks are adding new types of accounts
2 Apple is going to simplify its product line
3 Consumers have mixed feelings about supermarkets
4 When BMW bought Rover,
5 The new law will ban product placement
6 Following the launch of the Series 5 laptop, consumers were slow to understand
7 With this type of equipment in the US,

a product life cycles are so short that product launches are very frequent.
b its product positioning in relation to Psion's existing hardware products.
c it changed its product range towards more expensive cars.
d of cigarettes in movies.
e extending their product portfolio into financial services.
f and deliver fewer but more competitive models.
g to their product mix.

22.2 Look at the words in B opposite. Which applies to each of these products?

1 microwave ovens
2 cotton
3 cars
4 hamburgers
5 soap powder

22.3 Complete this marketer's description of his work using expressions from C opposite.

My name's Tomas. I'm Portuguese, and I've been (1) .... for Woof dog food for the whole of Portugal and Spain since I left business school last summer. The Woof (2) .... is owned by a big international group. The market for pet food in Portugal and Spain is growing very fast, as more and more people own dogs and cats, and we're trying to increase (3) .... of Woof through TV advertisements and hoardings in the street. Research shows that people have very positive ideas about it: it has a very positive (4) .... But the supermarkets have their (5) .... dog food, usually sold cheaper than our product, which is a problem. There are even (6) .... sold just under the name 'dog food'. We have to persuade people that it's worth paying a bit more for a (7) .... product like Woof, which is far better, of course.

Over to you

Have you seen any examples of product placement?

Do you know any products with strong brand images?

What are the advantages and disadvantages of brand name products, own brands and generics? Which do you prefer to buy?

23 Price

A Pricing

Our goods are **low-priced**. Permanently low **pricing** means we **charge** low prices all the time.

You mean **cheap**: your goods are poor quality. Our goods are **high-priced**, but we give customer service. And a lot of our goods are **mid-priced**: not cheap and not expensive.

Your goods are **expensive**. Customers don't need service.

You must be selling some goods **at cost** (what you pay for them) or **at a loss** (even less).

Yes. We have **loss leaders** – cheap items to attract customers in. But it's all below the 'official' **list price** or **recommended retail price**. We have a policy of **discounting**, selling **at a discount** to the list price.

If he goes on **undercutting** us, we can't stay in business.

B Word combinations with 'price'

	boom	a good period for sellers, when prices are rising quickly
	controls	government efforts to limit price increases
	cut	a reduction in price
price	hike	an increase in price
	war	when competing companies reduce prices in response to each other
	leader	a company that is first to reduce or increase prices
	tag	label attached to goods, showing the price; also means 'price'

C Upmarket and downmarket

Products, for example skis, exist in different **models**. Some are **basic**, some more **sophisticated**. The cheapest skis are **low-end** or **bottom-end**. The most expensive ones are **high-end** or **top-end** products, designed for experienced users (or people with a lot of money!). The cheapest **entry-level** skis are for beginners who have never bought skis before. Those in between are **mid-range**. If you buy sophisticated skis to replace basic ones, you **trade up** and move **upmarket**. If you buy cheaper skis after buying more expensive ones, you **trade down** and move **downmarket**.

Downmarket can show disapproval. If a publisher **takes** a newspaper **downmarket**, they make it more popular, but less cultural, to increase sales.

> BrE: upmarket, downmarket
> AmE: upscale, downscale

D Mass markets and niches

Mass market describes goods that sell in large quantities and the people who buy them. For example, family cars are a mass market product. A **niche** or **niche market** is a small group of buyers with special needs, which may be profitable to sell to. For example, sports cars are a niche in the car industry.

23.1 Look at the price list. Are the statements below true or false?

1 The pricing policy is to sell below list prices.
2 The Adagio is low-priced, and is cheaper than the competition.
3 The mid-priced models are the Brio and the Capricioso.
4 This retailer charges 16,908 euros for the Delicioso.
5 The Delicioso is the highest-priced model.
6 The Delicioso is cheaper than the competition.
7 All models are sold at a discount.

All prices in euros.

Model	List price	Our price	Competing product
Adagio	11,541	9,999	10,500
Brio	13,349	12,999	12,896
Capricioso	15,742	14,999	13,987
Delicioso	16,908	15,999	14,442

23.2 Complete the sentences with the appropriate form of words from B opposite.

1 A price .... by Mills may indicate the start of price increases by other producers.

2 Britain's house price .... has gone beyond London, with properties in Kent now worth 25 per cent more than a year ago.

3 Consumers will get price .... of eight per cent off phone bills from May.

4 When President Perez ended price ...., electricity, phone and transport costs went up.

5 Petron is a price ....; it's usually the first to offer lower prices.

6 The project had many design problems, pushing up the price .... for each helicopter from $11 million to $26 million.

7 There is a price .... between Easyjet and KLM on the London to Amsterdam route.

23.3 Correct the mistakes in italics, using expressions from C and D opposite.

I'm Denise van Beek, from sailing boat company Nordsee Marine. We have something for everyone. If you've never sailed before, try our (1) *mid-range* model, the Classic. It's six metres long and very easy to sail. After a year or two, many customers (2) *trade down* or (3) *take upmarket* to something more (4) *basic*, like the (5) *entry-level* nine-metre Turbosail, with more equipment and a bit more luxury. Our (6) *bottom end* product is the Fantasy. It's 15 metres long and has everything you need for comfort on long voyages. We also produce the Retro, a traditional boat. There's a small but profitable (7) *mass market* for this type of boat.

24 Place

Distribution: wholesalers, retailers and customers

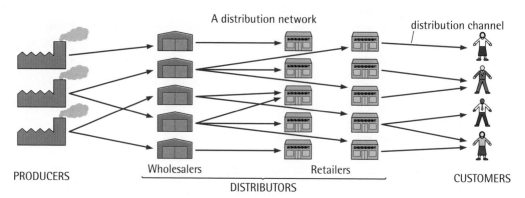

A distribution network

distribution channel

PRODUCERS | Wholesalers | Retailers | CUSTOMERS
DISTRIBUTORS

A **wholesaler** or shop selling a particular product, such as cars, is a **dealer**. A **reseller** sells computers. Wholesalers and retailers are **distributors**. Wholesalers are sometimes disapprovingly called **middlemen**.

B Shops

A **shop** (BrE) or **store** (AmE) is where people buy things. Companies may call it a **retail outlet** or **sales outlet**. Here are some types of shop:

- **chain store**: part of a group of shops, all with the same name.
- **convenience store**: small shop in a residential area and open long hours.
- **deep discounter**: a supermarket with very low prices.
- **department store**: very large shop with a wide variety of goods, usually in a town centre.
- **drugstore**: shop in a town centre in the US which sells medicines; you can also have coffee and meals there.
- **hypermarket**: very large shop with a wide variety of goods, usually outside a town.
- **supermarket**: very large shop, selling mainly food.

In Britain, a **shopping centre** or **shopping precinct** is a purpose-built area or building in a town centre with a number of shops. Outside towns, there are **shopping malls**, where it is easy to park.

Franchises are owned by the people that run them (**franchisees**), but they only sell the goods of one company. That company (the **franchisor**) provides goods, organizes advertising, and offers help and support. In return it takes a percentage of the profits of each franchisee. Many restaurants are also run like this.

C Direct marketing

Hi, I'm Beatrice and I work in a **direct marketing** company in Brussels. We organize **mailings** for many different products and services. This is **direct mail** but people often call it **junk mail**. We **target** our mailing lists very carefully: for example, we don't send **mailshots** for garden tools to people who live in apartments!

We also do **telemarketing**, selling by telephone, including **cold calls** to people who have had no contact with us before. People are often rude to the workers in our **call centres** when they do this.

> BrE: **call centre**
> AmE: **call center**

24.1 Use expressions from A opposite to complete this presentation.

Hi, my name's Michael Son. I started out in the PC business 15 years ago when I tried to buy a PC. There was a complicated (1) d............... c............... between the manufacturer and the customer: (2) w..................., (3) r................... and (4) r................... all added to the costs, but they didn't add much value from the (5) c..................'s point of view. Here at Son Computers, we manufacture every PC to order and deliver straight to the buyer. That way we cut out the (6) m................... .

24.2 Look at B opposite and say where you go if you want to:

1 park easily and visit different shops without going to the town centre.
2 visit different shops grouped together in a British town centre.
3 buy a packet of sugar when all the supermarkets are closed.
4 have a snack in an American city without going to a restaurant.
5 buy food very cheaply.
6 buy clothes in a town centre without going to a specialized clothes shop.

24.3 Which expression in C opposite does the 'it' in each sentence refer to?

1 *I really hate it, all that stuff coming through my letter box. It never stops.*

3 *300,000 well-targeted letters to cat-lovers? We can organize it, no problem.*

2 *It's a terrible place to work. We have to make 30 calls an hour, with few breaks.*

4 *I have to do it. I've never spoken to them before, but I've got no choice.*

5 *The two main activities that make it up are mailings and telemarketing.*

6 *People who come home to ten answerphone messages, all selling things, tend to hate it.*

A call centre

A Advertising

Each photo shows a different advertising **medium.**

Classified advertisements

Open air hoardings (BrE)/Billboards (AmE)

Neon signs

Display advertisements

TV commercial

Special display

The Internet is a new advertising medium.

Product endorsements are when famous people recommend a product.

A series of advertisements for a particular company or product is an **advertising campaign.** A person or business that **advertises** is an **advertiser.** An organization that designs and manages advertising campaigns is an **advertising agency.**

Sponsorship is where companies sponsor (pay some of the costs of) events like concerts and sports events.

> BrE: **ad, advert, advertisement**
> AmE: **ad, advertisement**

B The sales force

A company's **salespeople** (its **salesmen** and **saleswomen**) visit customers and persuade them to buy its products. Each member of this **salesforce** may be responsible for a particular region: his or her **sales area** or **sales territory.**

The head of the sales force is the **sales manager.**

C Promotional activities

Promotion (uncountable) is all the activities supporting the sale of a product, including advertising. **A promotion** (countable) describes:

- a **special offer** such as a **discount** or reduced price. (See Unit 23)

- a **free sample:** a small amount of the product to try or taste.

- a **free gift:** given with the product.

- **competitions** with **prizes.**

Supermarkets and airlines give **loyalty cards** to customers: the more you spend, the more points you get, and you can exchange these points for free goods or flights.

Cross-promotion is where you buy one product, and you are recommended to buy another product that may go with it.

25.1 Complete the crossword using expressions from A, B and C opposite.

Across
4 Better than a classified one. (7,13)
5 Free .... (7)
8 All the salespeople: sales .... (5)
10 An advertising .... organizes ads. (6)
11 Offers, competitions, etc. (10)
14 Given away free as part of a promotion. (5)
15 You win these in competitions. (6)
16 People or organizations who advertise. (11)
17 Female members of the sales force: sales
   .... (5)

Down
1 BrE for 'billboard'. (8)
3 One salesperson's region for selling. (9)
5 Electric advertising: neon .... (4)
6 Head of the sales force: sales .... (7)
7 Male salespeople. (8)
9 A new advertising medium. (8)
12 Television is an example of a .... (6)
13 Another word for 3 down (plural). (5)

25.2 Match the sentence (1–3) to the correct words (a–c).

1 Many supermarkets run competitions and offers to encourage people to buy from them.
2 For example, yesterday I bought two kilos of oranges for half the usual price.
3 I also bought some coffee, which came with a free mug.

a special offer
b promotions
c free gift

Over to you

What advertisements and promotional activities does your company or school use?

What advertising campaigns are famous in your country?

A The Internet

web address

banner advertisement

hyperlinks

web page

The **Internet service provider** or **ISP** is the organization that provides you with **Internet access**. You **register** and open an **account**, then they give you an email address so that you can communicate by **email** with other users. (See Unit 53) Some ISPs have their own **content** – news, information and so on – but many do not. After you **log on** by entering your **user name** and **password** (a secret word that only you know), you can **surf** to any **site** on the **World Wide Web**. If you're looking for a site about a particular subject, you can use a **search engine** like Google or Yahoo. When you've finished, remember to **log off** for **security** reasons.

B Clicks-and-mortar

My name's John, and I own a chain of sports shops. Last year, I started an **e-commerce** operation, selling goods over the Internet. We've done well. **Visitors** don't have trouble finding what they want, adding items to their **shopping cart** and paying for them **securely** by credit card. Last year we had two million **unique users** (different individual visitors) who generated 35 million **hits** or **page views**. That means our web pages were viewed a total of 35 million times!

E-commerce or **e-tailing** has even acted as a form of advertising and increased levels of business in our traditional **bricks-and-mortar** shops! Pure Internet commerce operations are very difficult. To succeed, I think you need a combination of **traditional retailing** and e-commerce: **clicks-and-mortar**. In our case, this has also helped us solve the **last mile problem**, the **physical delivery** of goods to Internet customers: we just deliver from our local stores!

C B2B, B2C and B2G

Selling to the public on the Internet is **business-to-consumer** or **B2C** e-commerce. Some experts think that the real future of e-commerce is going to be **business-to-business** or **B2B**, with firms ordering from suppliers over the Internet. This is **e-procurement**.

Businesses can also use the Internet to communicate with government departments, apply for government contracts and pay taxes: **business-to-government** or **B2G**.

26.1 Match the words you might see on a computer screen (1–6) with the activities you might be doing at that time (a–f).

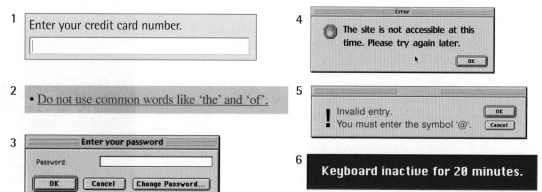

1 Enter your credit card number.

2 • Do not use common words like 'the' and 'of'.

3 Enter your password
Password:
OK   Cancel   Change Password...

4 Error
The site is not accessible at this time. Please try again later.
OK

5 Invalid entry.
You must enter the symbol '@'.
OK   Cancel

6 Keyboard inactive for 20 minutes.

a using a search engine
b logging on
c registering with an ISP

d typing an email address
e automatic logging off
f surfing and trying to enter a particular website

26.2 Find expressions in B opposite with the following meanings.

1 traditional shops (two possibilities)
2 selling on the Internet (two possibilities)
3 where you put your items before you purchase them
4 physical delivery of goods to Internet customers
5 how many times a web page is viewed

26.3 What type of e-commerce are the following? Choose from B2B, B2C, or B2G.

1 Private individuals can rent a car without going through a call centre.
2 The city is looking for construction companies to build a new airport. There are hundreds of pages of specifications you can obtain from the city authorities.
3 Car companies are getting together to buy components from suppliers in greater quantities, reducing prices.
4 Small businesses can get advice about wages, taxation, etc.
5 Members of the public can buy legal advice from law firms.
6 It can seem very convenient, but if you're out when the goods you ordered arrive at your house, you're in trouble!

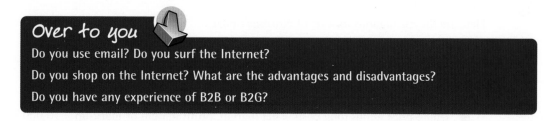

Over to you

Do you use email? Do you surf the Internet?

Do you shop on the Internet? What are the advantages and disadvantages?

Do you have any experience of B2B or B2G?

27 Sales and costs

A Sales 1

Sales describes what a business sells and the money it receives for it. Denise van Beek of Nordsee Marine is having a **sales meeting** with her **sales team**:

'Our **sales figures** and **turnover** (money received from sales) in the last year are good, with **revenue** (money from sales) of 14.5 million euros, on **volume** of 49 boats. This is above our **target** of 13 million euros. We estimate our **sales growth** next year at ten per cent, as the world economy looks good and there is demand for our products, so my **sales forecast** is nearly 16 million euros for next year. I'm relying on you!'

A sales meeting

B Sales 2

Here are some more uses of the word 'sale':

a **make a sale**: sell something
b **be on sale**: be available to buy
c **unit sales**: the number of things sold
d **Sales**: a company department
e **A sale**: a period when a shop is charging less than usual for goods
f **The sales**: a period when a lot of shops are having a sale

C Costs

The money that a business spends are its **costs**:

- **direct costs** are directly related to providing the product (e.g. salaries).
- **fixed costs** do not change when production goes up or down (e.g. rent, heating, etc.).
- **variable costs** change when production goes up or down (e.g. materials).
- **cost of goods sold** (**COGS**): the variable costs in making particular goods (e.g. materials and salaries).
- **indirect costs**, **overhead costs** or **overheads** are not directly related to production (e.g. adminstration).

Some costs, especially indirect ones, are also called **expenses**.

Costing is the activity of calculating costs. Amounts calculated for particular things are **costings**.

D Margins and mark-ups

Here are the calculations for one of Nordsee's boats:

- **selling price** = 50,000 euros
- **direct production costs** = 35,000 euros
- selling price minus direct production costs = **gross margin** = 15,000 euros
- **total costs** = 40,000 euros
- selling price minus total costs = **net margin, profit margin** or **mark-up** = 10,000 euros

The net margin or profit margin is usually given as a percentage of the selling price, in this case 20 per cent.

The mark-up is usually given as a percentage of the total costs, in this case 25 per cent.

27.1 Match the word combinations (1–7) to their definitions (a–f).

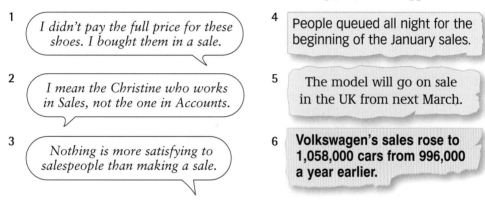

sales

1 figures

2 forecast

3 growth

4 revenue

5 target

6 turnover

7 volume

a money received from sales (2 expressions)

b sales aimed for in a particular period

c the number of things sold

d increase in sales

e statistics showing the amount sold

f sales predicted in a particular period

27.2 Match each use of the word 'sale' with the correct meaning (a–f) from B opposite.

1 *I didn't pay the full price for these shoes. I bought them in a sale.*

2 *I mean the Christine who works in Sales, not the one in Accounts.*

3 *Nothing is more satisfying to salespeople than making a sale.*

4 People queued all night for the beginning of the January sales.

5 The model will go on sale in the UK from next March.

6 Volkswagen's sales rose to 1,058,000 cars from 996,000 a year earlier.

27.3 Choose the correct expression from C opposite to describe Nordsee Marine's costs.

1 the salary of an office receptionist (direct / indirect cost)
2 heating and lighting of the building where the boats are made (fixed / variable cost)
3 the materials used in the boats, and the boatbuilders' salaries (overhead cost / COGS)
4 running the office (overhead / direct cost)
5 wood used in building the boats (fixed / variable cost)
6 the salary of a boatbuilder (direct / indirect cost)

27.4 Look at D opposite. Read what this company owner says and answer the questions.

'I'm Vaclav and I own a small furniture company in Slovakia. We make a very popular line of wooden chairs. Each costs 360 korunas to make, including materials and production. We estimate overheads, including administration and marketing costs, at 40 korunas for each chair, and we sell them to furniture stores at 500 korunas each.'

1 What is the gross margin for each chair?
2 What is the net margin for each chair?
3 What is the mark-up for each chair as a percentage of total costs?
4 What is the profit margin for each chair as a percentage of the selling price?

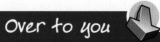

Over to you

Think of the company you work for or one you would like to work for. Which of its products or services has the highest sales? What are its biggest costs?

28 Profitability and unprofitability

A Profitable and unprofitable products

A supermarket manager talks about the costs and prices for some of its products.

Product	Cost per unit (euros)	Sale price per unit (euros)	Result
A	10	12	We **make a profit**: the product is **profitable** or **profit-making**.
B	15	15	We **break even**: we **reach break-even point**.
C	8	7	We make a **loss**. The product is **loss-making**, but we use Product C as a **loss leader** to attract people to the store, as we know they will then also buy profitable products.
D	12	22	Product D is very profitable and we sell a lot of it. It's one of our **money-spinners** or **cash cows**, products that have very good profitability.

B Budgets and expenditure

Like all companies, Nordsee and Vaclav have to **budget for**, or plan, their costs, and have a **budget**. Look at the graphs comparing their planned budgets with their **actual expenditure** (what they actually spent).

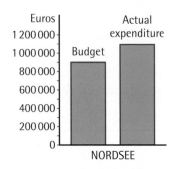

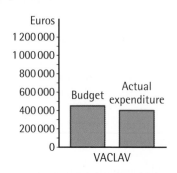

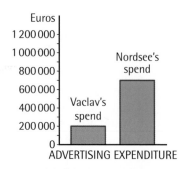

Nordsee went **over budget** and **overspent** by 200,000 euros.

Vaclav **underspent** by 50,000 euros. He was **under budget**.

On advertising, Vaclav's **spend** was only 200,000 euros, while Nordsee's advertising spend was 700,000.

Note: **Spend** is usually a verb, but it can also be a noun, as in **advertising spend**.

C Economies of scale and the learning curve

Ford is one of the biggest car companies in the world. It benefits from **economies of scale**. For example, the costs of developing a new car are enormous, but the company can spread them over a large number of cars produced and sold. In dealing with suppliers, it can obtain lower prices, because it buys in such large quantities.

The company also benefits from the **experience curve** or **learning curve**: as it produces more, it learns how to do things more and more quickly and efficiently. This brings down the cost of each thing produced, and the more they produce, the cheaper it gets.

28.1 Look at this information about Vaclav's products and answer the questions.

	Unit production cost (korunas)	Overheads per unit (korunas)	Selling price (korunas)	Number of units sold per year
Chairs	360	40	500	50,000
Stools*	180	20	195	70,000
Armchairs	700	70	800	20,000
Coffee tables	550	50	600	30,000
Dining tables	2500	300	3000	15,000

* chairs with three legs and no back

1 Which products make a profit?
2 Which product has the highest level of profitability as a percentage of its selling price?
3 Which loses money?
4 Which just breaks even?
5 Which is the biggest money-spinner or cash cow, in terms of overall profit?
6 Which product may be a loss leader, to encourage furniture stores to buy other, profitable products?

28.2 Complete the sentences using correct forms of expressions from B opposite.

1 She felt the organization was .... and wasting money on entertainment and luxury travel.

2 UK tobacco companies have an advertising .... of £50 million a year.

3 Orson Welles was supposed to make a film version of Heart of Darkness, but he ran ...., and the project was cancelled.

4 The repair budget for Windsor Castle after the fire was £40 million. In fact, the repairs were completed six months ahead of schedule and £3 million ....

5 Years of .... on investment in Britain's railways have left them in a very bad state.

6 Planning the concert, they found they had forgotten to .... the singers, and could only pay the orchestra.

7 Spending on books is rising as a proportion of total consumer ....

28.3 Match the sentence beginnings (1–3) with the correct endings (a–c). The sentences all contain expressions from C opposite.

1 There are economies of scale in hospital services;	a so cutting unit costs.
2 Some universities put more students into classes,	b but we are learning from our mistakes.
3 The learning curve is very steep,	c however, they only apply up to about 100–200 beds.

Over to you

Does your company, or one you would like to work for, have a cash cow or a loss leader?

Does your company, or one you would like to work for, benefit from economies of scale?

29 Getting paid

A Shipping and billing

When you ask to buy something, you **order** it, or **place an order for it**. When the goods are ready, they are **dispatched** or **shipped** to you.

An invoice is a document asking for payment and showing the amount to pay. The activity of producing and sending invoices is **invoicing** or **billing**.

B Trade credit

Vaclav is talking about his furniture business:

'Of course, we don't expect our business customers to pay immediately. They are given **trade credit**, a period of time before they have to pay, usually 30 or 60 days. If a customer orders a large quantity or pays within a particular time, we give them a **discount**, a reduction in the amount they have to pay.

But with some customers, especially ones we haven't dealt with before, we ask them to pay **upfront**, before they receive the goods.

Like all businesses, we have a **credit policy**, with **payment terms**: rules on when and how customers should pay. This is part of controlling **cash flow**, the timing of payments coming into and going out of a business.'

C Accounts

Jennifer and Kathleen are businesswomen. Jennifer has her own company in Britain and Kathleen owns one in the US.

The people and organizations we sell to are our customers or **accounts**. The most important ones are **key accounts**.

I'm waiting to be paid by some of my customers. These are my **debtors**. They **owe** me money.

The customers that I'm waiting to be paid by are my **accounts receivable** or **receivables**.

The suppliers and other organizations that I owe money to are my **creditors**. I must remember to pay tax to the **Inland Revenue** on time!

The suppliers and other organizations that I owe money to are my **accounts payable** or **payables**. I must remember to pay tax to the **Inland Revenue Service** on time!

Jennifer

Kathleen

There are some companies that owe me money, but I get the feeling I'm never going to get paid: they're **bad debts** and I've **written them off**.

29.1 Put these events in the correct order.

1 Messco dispatched the goods to Superinc.
2 Superinc ordered goods from Messco.
3 Superinc eventually settled the invoice.
4 Superinc did not pay the invoice on time.
5 Two weeks later, Superinc had still not received an invoice, making them think Messco's invoicing was not very efficient.
6 Someone in accounts at Messco chased the invoice by phoning the accounts department at Superinc.
7 When the goods arrived, Superinc noticed there was no invoice and asked Messco to issue one.
8 Messco's accounts department raised an invoice and sent it to Superinc.

29.2 Complete these sentences using expressions from B opposite.

1 .... is a constant problem. I get materials from suppliers on a 30-day payment basis, but I'm supplying large companies who pay me on a 60-day payment term.

2 With some types of new wine, you can pay a special price .... and wait for it to be delivered in about ten months' time.

3 Small businesses complain that larger companies abuse .... by paying invoices too slowly.

4 We offer a two per cent .... for payment within ten days.

5 We have a very strict ....: our .... are that everyone pays within 30 days.

29.3 Replace the underlined words with expressions from C opposite, using British English.

My name's Saleem and I own a clothing company. Our (1) most important customers are department stores. Getting paid on time is very important and we have an employee whose job is to chase (2) people who owe us money. Of course, we pay (3) suppliers and other people we owe money to as late as possible, except the (4) tax authorities, who we pay right on time! Luckily, I haven't had much of a problem with (5) people who don't pay at all, so we haven't had to (6) decide not to chase them any more.

Over to you

What are the normal payment terms in your company or the company you are interested in?

Do small companies have problems getting paid in your country? Do some businesses offer discounts to the public?

30 Assets, liabilities and the balance sheet

A Assets

An **asset** is something that has value, or the power to earn money. These include:

- **current assets**: money in the bank, investments that can easily be turned into money, money that customers owe, stocks of goods that are going to be sold.
- **fixed assets**: equipment, machinery, buildings and land.
- **intangible assets**: things which you cannot see. For example, **goodwill**: a company's good reputation with existing customers, and **brands** (See Unit 22): established brands have the power to earn money.

If a company is sold as **a going concern**, it has value as a profit-making operation, or one that could make a profit.

B Depreciation

Joanna Cassidy is head of IT (Information Technology) in a publishing company:

'Assets such as machinery and equipment lose value over time because they wear out, or are no longer up-to-date. This is called **depreciation** or **amortization**. For example, when we buy new computers, we **depreciate** them or **amortize** them **over** a very short period, usually three years, and a **charge** for this is shown in the financial records: the value of the equipment is **written down** each year and **written off** completely at the end.

The value of an asset at any one time is its **book value**. This isn't necessarily the amount that it could be sold for at that time. For example, land or buildings may be worth more than shown in the accounts, because they have increased in value. But computers could only be sold for less than book value.'

C Liabilities

Liabilities are a company's debts to suppliers, lenders, the tax authorities, etc. Debts that have to be paid within a year are **current liabilities**, and those payable in more than a year are **long-term liabilities**, for example bank loans.

D Balance sheet

A company's **balance sheet** gives a picture of its assets and liabilities at the end of a particular period, usually the 12-month period of its **financial year**. This is not necessarily January to December.

30.1 Look at A opposite. What kind of asset is each of the following? Which three are not assets?

1 Vans which a delivery company owns and uses to deliver goods.
2 Vans for sale in a showroom.
3 A showroom owned by a company that sells vans.
4 A showroom rented by a company that sells cars.
5 Money which customers owe, that will definitely be paid in the next 60 days.
6 Money which a bankrupt customer owes, that will certainly never be paid.
7 The client list of a successful training company, all of which are successful businesses.
8 The client list of a training company, with names of clients that have all gone bankrupt.

30.2 Use the correct forms of words in brackets from B opposite to complete these sentences.

1 The bank had lent too much and was left with a mountain of bad debts: £4.3 billion was .... (write off / wrote off / written off) last year.

2 Most highway building programs in the US are .... (amortization / amortize / amortized) over 30 years or more.

3 The company reported a record income of $251.2 million, after a $118 million .... (charge / charged / charges) for reduction in the .... (book value / books value / booked value) of its oil and gas properties.

4 Under the new law, businesses face five different .... (depreciate / depreciation / depreciations) rules for different types of equipment.

5 The company reported a loss of $12.8 million, partly due to a special charge of $1.5 million to .... (write down / wrote down / written down) the value of its spare parts inventory.

30.3 Look at C and D opposite and say if these statements are true or false.

1 Money that a company has to pay to a supplier in less than a year is a long-term liability.
2 A loan that a company has to repay to a bank over five years is a long-term liability.
3 A company's financial year can run from 1 May to 30 April.

Over to you

Obtain a copy of your company's balance sheet, or a copy of the balance sheet of a company that you are interested in. What are its main assets and liabilities?

You can find this information for companies all over the world at www.carol.co.uk (Company Annual Reports Online).

31 The bottom line

A

A Accounts

Hi, I'm Fiona and I'm an **accountant**. I work in Edinburgh for one of the big **accountancy firms**. We look at the financial records or **accounts** of a lot of companies. We work with the accountants of those companies, and the people who work under them: the **bookkeepers**. I like my profession: **accountancy**.

Sometimes we act as **auditors**: specialist outside accountants who **audit** a company's accounts, that is, we check them at the end of a particular period to see if they give a **true and fair view** (an accurate and complete picture). An **audit** can take several days, even for a fairly small company.

When a company's results are presented in a way that makes them look better than they really are, even if it follows the rules, it may be accused of **creative accounting** or **window dressing**. Of course, I never do this!

> The profession is called **accountancy** (BrE) or **accounting** (AmE). The activity is called **accounting** (BrE and AmE).

B Results

'A firm reports its performance in a particular period in its results. Results for a particular year are shown in the company's **annual report**. This contains, among other things, a **profit and loss account**.

In theory, if a company makes more money than it spends, it **makes a profit**. If not, it makes a **loss**. But it's possible for a company to show a profit for a particular period because of the way it presents its activities under the **accounting standards** or **accounting rules** of one country, and a loss under the rules of another. My firm operates in many countries and we are very aware of this!

A **pre-tax profit** or a **pre-tax loss** is one before tax is calculated. An **exceptional profit** or **loss** is for something that is not normally repeated, for example the sale of a subsidiary company or the costs of restructuring. (See Unit 34) A company's **gross profit** is before charges like these are taken away; its **net profit** is afterwards. The final figure for profit or loss is what people call informally the **bottom line**. This is what they really worry about!

If a company is making a loss, commentators may say that it is **in the red**. They may also use expressions with **red ink**, saying, for example, that a company is **bleeding red ink** or **haemorrhaging red ink**.'

> BrE: profit and loss account
> AmE: income statement

31.1 Look at A and B opposite to find the answers to the crossword.

Across

1 and 2 down What the British call the income statement. (6,3,4,7)

5 What accounts have to follow. (8)

6 Not occurring regularly. (11)

7 When companies announce results they .... them. (6)

11 The final figure for profit or loss. (6,4)

13 Another name for 'standard'. (4)

19 and 16, 18, 14 down What accounts should give. (4,3,4,4)

20 When things are made to look better than they really are. (6,8)

21 Known as accounting in the US. (11)

Down

2 See 1 across.

3 See 12 down.

4 Before tax is taken away. (3-3)

8 You find this in an annual report. (6)

9 Not a profit. (4)

10 Accounting that presents things in a positive light. (8)

12,3 down What Americans call the profit and loss account. (6,9)

14,16, 18 See 19 across.

17 Noun and verb related to 'auditor'. (5)

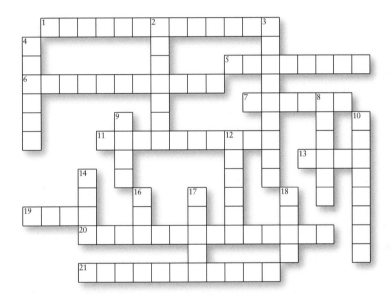

Over to you

Obtain a copy of your company's annual report, or the annual report of a company that you are interested in. Look at its profit and loss account (or income statement). What is the bottom line?

You can find this information for companies all over the world at www.carol.co.uk (Company Annual Reports Online).

32 Share capital and debt

A Capital

Capital is the money that a company uses to operate and develop. There are two main ways in which a company can **raise capital**, that is find the money it needs: it can use **share capital** or **loan capital**, from investors. These are people or organizations who **invest in** the company; they put money in hoping to make more money. (See Unit 36)

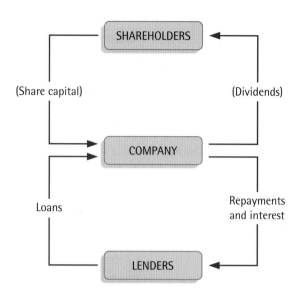

B Share capital

Share capital is contributed by **shareholders** who **put up money** and **hold shares** in the company. Each share represents ownership of a small proportion of the company. Shareholders receive periodic payments called **dividends**, usually based on the company's profit during the relevant period. Capital in the form of shares is also called **equity**.

A **venture capitalist** is someone who puts up money for a lot of new companies.

C Loan capital

Investors can also lend money, but then they do not own a small part of the company. This is **loan capital**, and an investor or a financial institution lending money in this way is a **lender**. The company borrowing it is the **borrower** and may refer to the money as **borrowing** or **debt**. The total amount of debt that a company has is its **indebtedness**.

The sum of money borrowed is the **principal**. The company has to pay **interest**, a percentage of the principal, to the borrower, whether it has made a profit in the relevant period or not.

D Security

Lending to companies is often in the form of **bonds** or **debentures**, loans with special conditions. One condition is that the borrower must have **collateral** or **security**: that is, if the borrower cannot repay the loan, the lender can take equipment or property, and sell it in order to get their money back. This may be an asset which was bought with the loan.

E Leverage

Many companies have both loan and share capital. The amount of loan capital that a company has in relation to its share capital is its **leverage**. Leverage is also called **gearing** in BrE. A company with a lot of borrowing in relation to its share capital is **highly leveraged** or **highly geared**. A company that has difficulty in making payments on its debt is **overleveraged**.

32.1 Choose the correct expressions in brackets from A, B and C opposite to complete the text.

I started 15 years ago with (1 capital/dividends) of $A50,000. We had one small restaurant in Sydney and now we have twenty throughout Australia. My (2 borrowers/shareholders) were members of my family: my parents, brothers and sisters all put up money. They didn't receive any (3 dividends/shares) for the first five years: we put all our profits back into the company! Now we want to increase the amount of
(4 equity/dividends), so we are looking for outside (5 borrowers/lenders).

(6 Lenders/Shareholders) have been very helpful. We obtained $A50,000 of (7 loan capital/share capital) from a bank when we started. Now we have paid off all the (8 dividends/principal) and (9 interest/ shares) after seven years. We have taken out other loans recently, but our (10 lending/indebtedness) is not bad in relation to the size of the business.

32.2 Answer these questions, using expressions from C, D and E opposite.

1 You want to raise money for your company, but you do not want to sell shares. What can you use instead? (2 expressions)
2 You want to raise money and you want to reassure lenders that they will get their money back if your company cannot repay. What would you offer them? (2 expressions)
3 You are interviewed by a financial journalist who wants to know why you are borrowing money. What do you tell them that you want to increase? (2 words)
4 The journalist writes an article saying that your company has a lot of debt in relation to its share capital. Which two expressions might she use in her article?
5 A few months later the journalist writes an article saying that your company has too much debt in relation to its ability to pay. Which expression might she use in her article?

Over to you

Would you like to start a business? What sort? Where would you get the capital?

Where do people in your country normally get capital? What are the advantages and disadvantages of the different methods?

33 Success and failure

Cash mountains and surpluses

Predaco is a successful company. Over the years, it has **distributed** some profits or **earnings** to shareholders, but it has also kept profits in the form of **retained earnings** and built up its **cash reserves**; it is sitting on a **cash pile** or **cash mountain**. These reserves may be used for investment or to make **acquisitions**: to buy other companies. (See Unit 34)

Debt and debt problems

Here are some expressions that can be used to talk about a company's debts, or a country's foreign debts:

debt	repayment servicing	when a company repays its debt and/or interest on it; 'debt repayment' describes a particular amount repaid
	burden	a company's debt, especially when considered as a problem
	crisis	when a company has serious difficulty repaying its debt
	rescheduling restructuring	when a company persuades lenders to change repayment dates and terms
	default	when a company fails to make a debt repayment

Note:

to
reschedule
restructure
} a debt

to
repay
default on
service
} a debt

Turnarounds and bailouts

Doomco is in financial trouble and it is being described as **sick**, **ailing** and **troubled**. They've called in a company doctor, Susan James, an expert in **turning round** companies. There may be a **turnaround** and Doomco may recover. But if there is no **recovery**, the company may **collapse** completely. Ms James is currently looking for another company to **bail out** Doomco by buying it. This would be a **bailout**.

Bankruptcy

If a company is in serious financial difficulty, it has to take certain legal steps.

In the US, it may ask a court to give it time to reorganize by **filing for bankruptcy protection** from **creditors**, the people it owes money to.

In Britain, a company that is insolvent, i.e. unable to pay its debts, may **go into administration**, under the management of an outside specialist called an **administrator**.

If the company cannot be saved, it **goes into liquidation** or **into receivership**. Receivers are specialists who sell the company's assets and pay out what they can to creditors. When this happens, a company is **wound up**, and it **ceases trading**.

A company in difficulty that cannot be saved **goes bankrupt**.

33.1 Match the sentence beginnings (1–6) with the correct endings (a–f). The sentences all contain expressions from A opposite.

1 For a group sitting on a cash mountain of £2 billion, GEC's sale of
2 The group had a cash pile of nearly £300 million at the end of March
3 The airline has built its cash reserves
4 MCA's earnings for the fourth quarter rose 26 per cent to $21.8 million,
5 Raytheon has announced the $2.9 billion acquisition
6 The UK tax system encourages the distribution of earnings

a because of higher revenue from home video and pay TV.
b to finance plans for global expansion.
c to shareholders, rather than encouraging companies to invest.
d of Texas Instruments' defence electronics business.
e – plenty of money for acquisitions.
f Satchwell to Siebe for £80 million will make little difference.

33.2 Complete the sentences with expressions from B and C opposite. There may be more than one answer.

1 Our economy could .... under its huge debt .... – we owe $100 billion to foreign investors and banks alone.

2 The railway company made a profit of 140 billion yen, even after paying out 300 billion yen in debt ....

3 MidWest bank has made a strong .... from the dark days of the farm debt crisis.

4 The IMF's .... might not be enough to pull the country back from debt ....

5 Mr Owen, chairman of Energis, is to receive a bonus of nearly £900,000 for his work in .... round the .... company.

33.3 Rachel is an accountant. Correct the mistakes in italics, using expressions from D opposite.

> I work in the corporate recovery department of a London accountancy firm, with companies that are in financial difficulty. They may be in (1) *administer*, and we try to find ways of keeping them in operation. We may sell parts of the company and this, of course, means laying people off.
>
> Our US office works with a system where a company in difficulty can get (2) *protectors* from (3) *credit*, giving it time to reorganize, and pay off debts.
>
> If the company can't continue as a going concern, it (4) *goes into receivers*: we (5) *wind off* the company and it (6) *ends business*. We sell the assets and divide the money up among the creditors in a process of (7) *liquification*.

Over to you

Do you think the government should bail out loss-making companies to avoid making people unemployed?

34 Mergers, takeovers and sell-offs

A Stakes and joint ventures

a stake an interest a holding	in a company	the shares that one investor has in a company
a majority	stake interest holding	when more than 50 per cent of the shares of a company are owned by one investor, giving them control over how it is run
a minority	stake interest holding	when an investor owns less than 50 per cent of the shares of a company

Two companies may work together in a particular area by forming an **alliance** or **joint venture**; they may remain separate companies, or form a new company in which they both have a stake.

B Mergers and takeovers

General Oil and PP have announced they are going to merge. It will be the biggest ever **merger** in the oil industry.

Abbot Bank is doing badly, and may become the victim of a **predator**. There were rumours of a possible takeover by Bullion, but it says it won't play the **white knight** for Abbot by coming to its defence. This leaves Abbot exposed to **acquisition**, and it may be **prey** to a big international bank. Abbot does have a **poison pill** however, in the form of a special class of shares that will be very expensive for a predator to buy.

Blighty Telecom is to split into two, and demerge its fixed-line and mobile businesses as part of on-going **restructuring**. The aim of the demerger is to cut debt by £10 billion.

Ciments de France, the French building group, is to **acquire** Red Square Industries of the UK for 3.1 billion euros. This is a **friendly bid**, as RSI are likely to welcome it and agree to it. But the takeover comes only a year after RSI rejected a **hostile bid**, an unwanted one.

C Conglomerates

Cotton makes a series of acquisitions of retail and non-retail businesses, and becomes the **parent company** in a **conglomerate** or **combine**, with the other businesses as its **subsidiaries**.

1990s

1985

2000

Low-price general retail Cotton Stores acquires Bestco supermarkets and **diversifies into** food retailing.

Shareholders complain that Cotton Group is **unfocused**. They demand that its CEO should **dispose of** non-retail companies, which they describe as **non-core assets**, and reinvest the money in its main, **core activity**: retailing. They say that this **divestment** and **restructuring** is necessary for future growth and profitability.

34.1 Match the sentence beginnings (1–5) with the correct endings (a–e). The sentences all contain expressions from A and B opposite.

1 The Canadian government decided to sell 45 per cent
2 UK Gold is a successful satellite channel
3 Russia's second biggest airline is trying to buy a stake
4 China signed an agreement to develop a regional jet, setting up a joint
5 Mr Sugar's majority holding in Amstrad

a made him the UK's 15th richest person.
b of the state airline to the public, and keep a 55 per cent majority stake.
c in which the BBC has a minority interest.
d in its US counterpart so they can work out a marketing alliance.
e venture company in which it will have a 46 per cent stake, Airbus 39 per cent, and Singapore Technologies 15 per cent.

34.2 Which expressions in B do the underlined words in these headlines refer to?

1
ABC INVITES APPROACHES
The financially troubled ABC company has in effect put itself up for sale …

2
BREAKING UP IS HARD TO DO
Unhappy investors in W H Smith have been asking its managers to break up the retail group …

3
CLYDE REJECTS 'INADEQUATE' OFFER BY GULF CANADA
Clyde Petroleum's board yesterday asked shareholders to reject what it called a 'wholly inadequate' offer …

4
EAGLES SWOOP ON SHARKS
Eagles, which owns Sheffield Eagles Rugby team, has bought a 40 per cent stake in Sheffield Sharks Basketball club …

5
GLOBAL STORES ON THE LOOK-OUT
Following its acquisition of seven retailers in Europe in the last five years, GS is on the hunt for …

6
REED ELSEVIER IN £20 BILLION LINK-UP WITH WOLTERS KLUWER
Reed UK is set to become part of an international group with headquarters in the Netherlands …

34.3 Use expressions from C opposite to complete what this journalist says about conglomerates.

A company that has (1) d................. may decide to limit its activities by selling those (2) s................. that do not fit in with its overall strategy. The board of the (3) p................. c................. may talk about (4) d................. and (5) r................., and getting out of particular businesses. In this case, the group (6) d................. o................. its (7) n.................- c................. a................. and uses the money to invest in and concentrate on its (8) c................. activities.

Over to you

Are mergers and takeovers common in your country?
Think of a famous merger or takeover that you found interesting. Was it successful?

35 Personal finance

A Traditional banking

'I'm Lisa. I have an **account** at my local **branch** of one of the big **high-street banks**. I have a **current account** for writing cheques, paying by **debit card** and paying bills. It's a **joint account** with my husband. Normally, we're **in the black**, but sometimes we spend more money than we have in the account and we **go into the red**. This **overdraft** is agreed by the bank up to a maximum of £500, but we pay quite a high **interest rate** on it.

BrE: cheque; AmE: check

I also have a **deposit account** or **savings account** for keeping money longer term. This account pays us **interest** (but not very much, especially after tax!).

We have a **credit card** with the same bank too. Buying with **plastic** is very convenient. We **pay off** what we spend each month, so we don't pay interest. The interest rate is even higher than for overdrafts!

Like many British people, we have a **mortgage**, a loan to buy our house.'

> BrE: current account, cheque account
> AmE: checking account

B New ways of banking

'My name's Kevin. I wasn't happy with my bank. There was always a queue, and on the **bank statement** that they sent each month they took money out of my account for **banking charges** that they never explained. So I moved to a bank that offers **telephone banking**. I can phone them any time to check my **account balance** (the amount I have in my account), **transfer** money to other accounts and pay bills.

Now they also offer **Internet banking**. I can **manage my account** sitting at my computer at home.'

C Personal investing

Lisa again:

'We have a savings account at a **building society** which is going to be **demutualized** (See Unit 12) and turned into a bank with shareholders. All the members will get a **windfall,** a special once-only payment of some of the society's assets to its members.

We have some **unit trusts**, shares in **investment companies** that put money from **small investors** like me into different companies. My cousin in the US calls unit trusts **mutual funds.**

I also pay **contributions** into a **private pension,** which will give me a regular income when I stop working. I've never joined a **company pension scheme** and the government **state pension** is very small!'

35.1 Look at A opposite and say if these statements are true or false.

1 You talk about the local 'agency' of a high-street bank.
2 Americans refer to current accounts as check accounts.
3 A joint account is held by more than one person.
4 If you put 10,000 euros into a new account and spend 11,000 euros, you have an overdraft of 1,000 euros and you are 1,000 euros in the red.
5 An account for saving money is called a safe account.
6 An account that pays a lot of interest has a high interest rate.
7 If you pay for something with a credit card, you can say, informally, that you use plastic to pay for it.
8 If you pay the complete amount that you owe on a credit card, you pay it down.

35.2 Kevin is phoning his bank. What expressions in A and B opposite could replace each of the underlined items?

1 I want to <u>swap</u> £500 from my savings account to my <u>ordinary account,</u> because I don't want to have <u>the situation where I've spent more than I've put in.</u>
2 How much is in my savings account? What's the <u>amount in there at the moment?</u>
3 On the savings account, what's the <u>percentage</u> you pay to savers every year?
4 How much <u>extra money have you added</u> to my savings account in the last three months?
5 On the last <u>list of the all the money going out of and coming into the account,</u> there's <u>an amount that you've taken off the account</u> that I don't understand.

35.3 Match the sentence beginnings (1–3) with the correct endings (a–c). The sentences all contain expressions from C opposite.

1 Investment companies are reporting a sharp increase in the number of
2 Consumers are using their windfall gains from building society
3 Peter is 26 and is wondering whether to join his company pension scheme. He would contribute a small percentage of his salary and his employer would make an equivalent contribution.

a If he decides to stay for at least two years he should join. If not, he should take out a personal pension.
b small investors who are investing in unit trusts.
c demutualizations to buy new furniture or a new car.

Over to you

What type of bank accounts and personal investments do you prefer?

What are the advantages and disadvantages of the different types?

36 Financial centres

A Financial centres

Financial centres are places where there are many banks and other **financial institutions**. London as a financial centre is called **the City** or **the Square Mile**, and New York is **Wall Street**.

Financial centres bring together **investors** and the businesses that need their investment. A **speculator** is an investor who wants to make a quick profit, rather than invest over a longer period of time.

Brokers, **dealers** and **traders** buy and sell for investors and in some cases, for themselves or the organizations they work for.

BrE: centre; AmE: center

B Stock markets

Heather Macdonald of Advanced Components:

'We needed more capital to expand, so we decided to **float** the company (sell shares for the first time) in a **flotation**. Our **shares** were **issued**, and **listed** (BrE and AmE) or **quoted** (BrE only) for the first time on the **stock market**. Because we are a UK-based company, we are listed on the London **stock exchange**.

Stock markets in other countries are also called **bourses**. Maybe when our company is really big, we'll issue more shares on one of the European bourses!'

Note: You can write **stock market** or **stockmarket**; one or two words.

BrE: **shares / stocks** (countable) **and shares**
AmE: **stock** (uncountable)

C Other financial markets

Other financial products include:

- **commercial paper**: short-term lending to businesses.
- **bonds**: longer-term lending to businesses and the government.
- **currencies** (**foreign exchange** or **forex**): buying and selling the money of particular countries.
- **commodities**: metals and farm products.

These are traded directly between dealers by phone and computer. Commodities are also traded in a **commodities exchange**. Shares, bonds and commercial paper are **securities**, and the financial institutions that deal in them are **securities houses**.

D Derivatives

A **futures contract** is an agreement giving an obligation to sell a fixed amount of a security or commodity at a particular price on a particular future date.

An **options contract** is an agreement giving the right, but not the obligation, to buy or sell a security or commodity at a particular price at a particular future time, or in a period of future time.

These contracts are **derivatives**. Dealers guess how the price of the **underlying** security or commodity will change in the future, and use derivatives to try to buy them more cheaply.

36.1 Correct the eight mistakes in italics in this article, using expressions from A opposite.

Now that a lot of buying and selling can be done over computer networks, (1) *breakers* and (2) *tradesmen* do not need to be in one place, and (3) *speculists* can make money dealing from a computer in their living room.

In New York, the area around (4) *the South Bronx* is traditionally home to many financial institutions, such as the New York Stock Exchange. But many of them have now moved some or all of their offices outside this expensive area.

ndon

New York

London is one of Europe's most important financial (5) *towns*: over 500 foreign banks have offices in London, and its stock exchange is the largest in Europe. But more and more financial (6) *institutes* are not actually based in the traditional area of the (7) *Citadel* or (8) *Mile Square*. As in New York, they are moving to areas where property is cheaper.

So, will financial centres continue to be as important in the future as they are now?

36.2 Look at B opposite and say if these statements are true or false.

1 'Stocks' is another name for shares.
2 'Stock market' means the same as 'stock exchange'.
3 Bourses are only found in France.
4 An American would normally talk about shares 'quoted' on the New York Stock Exchange.
5 Shares in Company X are being sold for the first time. This is a flotation.

36.3 Use expressions from C and D opposite to describe:

1 a bank that makes companies' shares available.
2 a contract to buy 500 tons of wheat for delivery in three months.
3 coffee and copper.
4 dollars, euros and yen.
5 lending to a company for less than a year.
6 lending to a local government authority in the form of 10-year investment certificates.
7 shares and bonds, but not currencies or commodities.
8 the London Metals Exchange.
9 the right to buy shares in a company in one month, at 150 pence per share.

Over to you

What is your country's main financial centre? Is it in the capital or another city?

What are the advantages and disadvantages of different securities and commodities, and ways of dealing?

37 Trading

A Market indexes

If there is **demand** for shares in a company, for example because it is doing well, its **share price** goes up. If not, its price goes down. The overall value of shares traded on a stock market is shown by an **index** (plural: **indexes** or **indices**). Some of the main ones are:

1 London: FTSE (pronounced 'Footsie'): the Financial Times Stock Exchange index.
2 New York: the Dow Jones Industrial Average ('the Dow'). Especially long-established 'old economy' companies.
3 New York: NASDAQ. Especially hi-tech 'new economy' companies.
4 Paris: CAC 40.
5 Frankfurt: DAX.
6 Hong Kong: Hang Seng.
7 Tokyo: Nikkei.

B Market activity: good times ...

Trading has been heavy on the New York Stock Exchange, with **very high turnover** of one and a half billion shares **changing hands**. We've seen **spectacular gains**, especially among **blue chips**.

'Translation'
= buying and selling of shares ...
= large number ...
= being bought and sold ...
= big increases in value ... famous companies with history of profit in good and bad economic times

This **bull market** seems set to continue, after yesterday's **record high** at the **close**. Dealers seem **bullish** and expect the Dow **to go through** the 15,000 **barrier** soon.

= rising prices ...

= highest level ever ...
= end of the working day ...
= optimistic ...
= to pass the 'round' number of ...

C ... and bad times

There was **panic selling** on the New York Stock Exchange today as prices fell to **new five-year lows**. We've seen some **spectacular declines**, with billions of dollars **wiped off** the **value** of some of America's best-known companies, and more than **10 per cent of total market capitalization**.
The **bear market** continues, with prices set to fall further in the next few days. Dealers are **bearish**, with many saying there is no sign of **a rally**. If prices continue to fall, there may be another **stock market collapse** or **crash**, like the ones in 1929 and 1987.

'Translation'
= selling shares for any price ...
= their lowest point for five years ...
= large decreases ...
= taken off the total share value ...
= the total value of shares listed on the market going down by 10 per cent ...
= falling prices ...

= pessimistic ...

= prices starting to rise again ...

= very serious drop in the value of shares on the market, with serious economic consequences ...

Note: The following words have a similar meaning.

Verb	Noun
to rally	a rally
to recover	a recovery

37.1 Complete this financial report using expressions from A opposite.

Yesterday in Asia, in (1) .... , the Hang Seng closed 1.6 per cent up at 15,657 exactly. In Tokyo the (2) .... was also up, at 15,747.20. In (3) .... last night, the (4) .... closed 1.8 per cent higher at 10,824 exactly, and the hi-tech (5) .... index was 3.3 per cent up at 3,778.32. Turning now to Europe, in early trading in (6) .... the FTSE is 0.1 per cent down at 6,292.80. The French (7) .... index is also slightly down at 6,536.85. The (8) .... in Germany, however, is 0.1 per cent higher at 6,862.85.

37.2 Use expressions from B opposite to describe:

1 shares in companies like IBM, Kodak, and Procter and Gamble.
2 buying and selling of shares on a stock market.
3 a day with twice as many shares sold as usual on a particular stock market.
4 shares that were worth $15 and are now worth $110.
5 a period when the stock market index has gone from 20,000 to 25,000.
6 the feelings of dealers who are optimistic that prices will continue to rise.
7 when a stock market index reaches 25,500 for the first time.
8 the level on a stock market index which may be difficult for shares to pass.

37.3 Complete these headlines with expressions from C opposite.

1
TECHNOLOGY STOCKS SEE BIG ....

2
**SHARES CONTINUE TO SLIDE: ....
MARKET MAY END IN ....**

3
SHARE PRICES AT TWO-YEAR ....

4
DEALERS .... AS MARKET
SENTIMENT CONTINUES TO WORSEN

5
.... *AS INVESTORS
RUSH TO SELL AT ANY PRICE*

6
PRICES CONTINUE TO FALL
WITH NO SIGN OF ....
ON THE HORIZON

7
BILLIONS ....
OFF SHARES IN
NERVOUS TRADING

Over to you

Is it usual in your country for ordinary people to own shares? Do people follow the stock market closely?

38 Indicators 1

A Finance and economics

Finance is:

- money provided or lent for a particular purpose.
- the management of money by countries, organizations or people.
- the study of money management.

High finance involves large amounts of money used by governments and large companies. A person's or organization's **finances** are the money they have and how it is managed, etc. The related adjective is **financial**.

Economics is:

- the study of how money works and is used.
- calculations of whether a particular activity will be profitable.

Related adjectives: a profitable activity is **economic**; an unprofitable one is **uneconomic**. If something is **economical**, it is cheap to buy, to use or to do. If not, it is **uneconomical**.

Economic indicators (see B, C and D below) are figures showing how well a country's **economy** (economic system) is working.

B Inflation and unemployment

Inflation is rising prices, and the rate at which they are rising is the **inflation rate**. The related adjective is **inflationary**.

The **unemployed** are people without jobs in a particular area, country, etc. The level of **unemployment** is the number of people without a job. Unemployed people are **out of work**, and are also referred to as **jobless** (adj.) or **the jobless**.

C Trade

The **balance of payments** is the difference between the money coming into a country and that going out. The **trade balance** is the difference between payments for imports (goods and services from abroad) and payments for **exports** (products and services sold abroad). When a country exports more than it imports, it has a **trade surplus**. When the opposite is the case, it has a **trade deficit**. The amount of this surplus or deficit is the **trade gap**.

D Growth and GDP

Economic output is the value of goods and services produced in a country or area. **Gross domestic product** or **GDP** is the value of all the goods and services produced in a particular country.

The size of an economy is also sometimes measured in terms of **gross national product** or **GNP**. This also includes payments from abroad, for example, from investments.

Growth is when output in the economy increases. The **growth rate** is the speed at which a company's economy **grows** and gets bigger.

38.1 Complete these sentences with expressions from A opposite.

1 Eating pasta, potatoes and rice rather than meat and fish is ....

2 Buying your food at a small local shop rather than at a big supermarket is ....

3 Someone who arranges multibillion-dollar loans to governments works in ....

4 Someone who is heavily in debt has problematic ....

5 If you obtain money for investment in a business project, you raise ....

6 Someone who teaches about trade between countries is a teacher of ....

7 Pig farming is at present unprofitable and ....

38.2 Complete what this reporter says about Paradiso's economy with expressions from B and C opposite.

Paradiso's economic indicators are perfect. In the past, Paradiso imported more than it exported, and there was a (1) ....: this (2) .... was very worrying. Now the country exports a lot of computer equipment, but still imports most of its food: the value of (3) .... is more than the value of (4) ...., so there is a (5) .... and the (6) .... is positive. Prices are rising very slowly: with an (7) .... of two per cent per year, (8) .... is under control. Of the working population, very few are (9) ....: only three per cent are (10) ....

38.3 Look at D opposite and complete the graph and the pie charts using the information below.

The growth rate in Paradiso was around four per cent a year for ten years. A period of very fast growth followed, with the growth rate reaching 12 per cent ten years later. Growth was nine per cent in the following three years, but fell to two per cent in the year after that. It then increased steadily to reach five per cent two years ago, and has stayed at that level.

30 years ago, GDP in Paradiso came 70 per cent from agriculture, 20 per cent from industry and 10 per cent from services. At that time, GDP was US$1,000 per person in terms of today's dollars.

Today, GDP per person is US$10,000, coming 50 per cent from industry, 40 per cent from services and 10 per cent from agriculture.

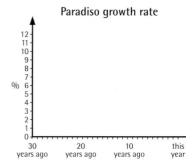

Paradiso growth rate

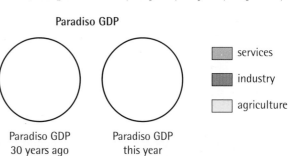

Paradiso GDP

Paradiso GDP
30 years ago

Paradiso GDP
this year

services

industry

agriculture

Over to you

What is the current economic situation of your country? In what ways is the government trying to influence it?

39 Indicators 2

A Going up

You use a number of verbs to describe amounts or figures going up.

1 **BT SHARES <u>ADVANCE</u> IN ACTIVE TRADING** = Shares in BT increased in value.

2 **TRADE SURPLUS <u>JUMPS</u> TO RECORD LEVEL** = The value of exports over imports has gone up quickly.

3 **PETROL PRICES SET TO <u>SKYROCKET</u>** = Petrol prices are going to rise by a lot.

4 **UNEMPLOYMENT <u>LEAPS</u> TO TEN-YEAR HIGH** = The number of people without work has gone up quickly.

5 **YAHOO! <u>SOARS</u> AS INTERNET EXPLOSION CONTINUES** = Shares in Yahoo! have increased greatly in value.

6 **VW PROFITS UP AS CAR SALES CONTINUE TO <u>SURGE</u>** = Profits in VW have increased thanks to rapidly rising car sales.

B Going down

You also use a number of verbs to describe amounts or figures going down.

7 **1,000 JOBS <u>AXED</u> AS DEFENCE PLANT CLOSES** = A defence company has told 1,000 factory employees that they are to lose their jobs.

8 **EUROPEAN CENTRAL BANK <u>CUTS</u> RATE IN SURPRISE MOVE** = The ECB has reduced interest rates.

9 **MEGACORP <u>EASES</u> ON PROFITS WARNING** = Megacorp's share price has gone down slightly after they said that profits would be lower than expected.

10 **SEPTEMBER RETAIL SALES <u>PLUMMET</u>** = Sales in shops have fallen a lot in September.

11 **GOVERNMENT <u>SLASHES</u> INCOME TAX TO TEN PER CENT** = The government has reduced income tax by a large amount.

12 **EURO <u>DIVES</u> TO NEW LOWS** = The euro currency has fallen to its lowest value ever.

C Peaks and troughs

If a figure rises to a level and then stops rising, remaining at that level, it **levels off** and **remains steady** or **stable**.

If a figure reaches its highest level – a **peak** – and then goes down, it **peaks** at that level. If it reaches its lowest level – a **trough** – and then **bottoms out**, it falls to that level and then starts rising again.

D Boom and bust

Demand is the amount of goods and services that people want in a particular period.

A **boom** is when there is rising demand, and other indicators are strong.

Stagnation is when the economy is growing slowly, or not at all.

Stagflation is when slow growth is combined with prices that are increasing fast.

Recession is a period when there is **negative growth,** a period when the economy is producing less. A **slump** is a very bad recession. A **depression** is a very bad slump.

39.1 Look at these headlines containing words from A and B opposite and say whether the statements about them are true or false.

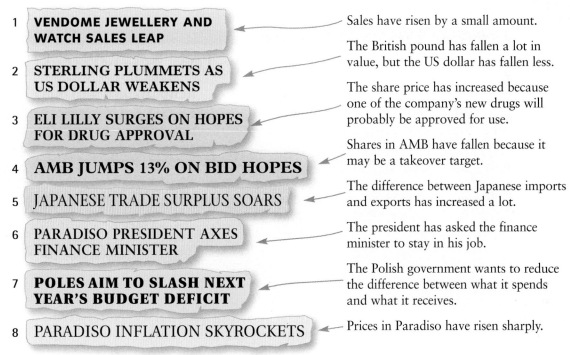

1 **VENDOME JEWELLERY AND WATCH SALES LEAP** — Sales have risen by a small amount.

2 **STERLING PLUMMETS AS US DOLLAR WEAKENS** — The British pound has fallen a lot in value, but the US dollar has fallen less.

3 **ELI LILLY SURGES ON HOPES FOR DRUG APPROVAL** — The share price has increased because one of the company's new drugs will probably be approved for use.

4 **AMB JUMPS 13% ON BID HOPES** — Shares in AMB have fallen because it may be a takeover target.

5 JAPANESE TRADE SURPLUS SOARS — The difference between Japanese imports and exports has increased a lot.

6 PARADISO PRESIDENT AXES FINANCE MINISTER — The president has asked the finance minister to stay in his job.

7 **POLES AIM TO SLASH NEXT YEAR'S BUDGET DEFICIT** — The Polish government wants to reduce the difference between what it spends and what it receives.

8 PARADISO INFLATION SKYROCKETS — Prices in Paradiso have risen sharply.

39.2 Complete the crossword with expressions from C and D opposite.

Across
1 The worst possible economic situation. (10)
5 Inflation .... when it reaches its highest level. (5)
9 When unemployment stays at its highest it .... (6,3)
11 When output starts rising from its lowest level it .... (7,3)

Down
2 A period when the economy is not healthy. (9)
3 Worse than 2 down, but not as bad as 1 across. (5)
4 During a recession, there is .... growth. (8)
6 Rising prices without rising growth. (11)
7 A very slow economy. (10)
8 If inflation doesn't change, it remains .... (6)
10 A very positive economic situation. (4)

Over to you

Think about a company or country that you know. How well has it performed in the last few years?

40 Wrongdoing and corruption

A Wrongdoing

PARADISO FINANCIAL SERVICES
REGULATORY AUTHORITY

*We **regulate** financial services; our job is to prevent financial **wrongdoing** and punish the **wrongdoers**.*

> **Insider dealing** or **insider trading**: someone buys or sells securities using information that is not publicly available. **Chinese walls** are measures that you can take to stop knowledge in one department of your company being illegally used by another department, to buy or sell shares for example.

> **Price fixing**: a group of companies in the same market secretly agree to fix prices at a certain level, so they do not have to compete with each other.

> **Market rigging**: a group of investors work together to stop a financial market functioning as it should, to gain an advantage for themselves.

B Bribery and corruption

An illegal payment to persuade someone to do something is a **bribe**, or informally a **backhander** (BrE only), **kickback** or **sweetener**. To **bribe** someone is **bribery**. Someone who receives bribes is **corrupt** and involved in **corruption**. This is informally known as **sleaze**, especially in politics.

C Fraud and embezzlement

'I'm Sam Woo. I've been a **fraud squad** detective for 20 years and I've seen a lot!

Once, a gang **counterfeited** millions of banknotes in a garage. We found US$10 million in **counterfeit notes**. They were very good quality. **Counterfeiting** or **forgery** of banknotes was a problem, but now all the **forgers** are in jail.

Faking luxury goods like Rolex watches was also a problem, but we're working hard to close workshops where **fakes** are made.

There have been bad cases of **fraud** where someone offers to lend money, but demands that the borrower pays a "fee" before they get the loan. People can be stupid.

And there's **embezzlement**, a type of fraud where someone illegally gets money from their employer. One accountant sent false invoices to the company he worked for, and paid money from his company into bank accounts of false companies he had "created". He **embezzled** $2 million – quite a **scam**.

There used to be a lot of **racketeers** demanding "protection money" from businesses. If they didn't pay, their businesses were burnt down.

Money laundering, hiding the illegal origin of money, is common – gangsters buy property with money from drugs. When they sell the property, the money becomes "legal". But banks now help by telling us when someone makes a large cash deposit.'

40.1 Answer the questions using expressions from A and B opposite.

1 Two ferry companies with ferries on the same route secretly meet in order to decide the prices they will charge next summer. What are they guilty of?

2 A company that wants to keep its share price high makes secret payments to investors who buy its shares. What are the company and the investors guilty of?

3 A rich businessman lends $1 million to a politician so that he can buy a house. The politician pays no interest on the loan and does not mention it when asked to give a complete account of his finances. Which word, used especially about politicians, do people use to talk about this?

4 Specialists in one department of a financial institution are advising Company X on a merger with another company. In another department of the financial institution, traders hear about this and buy large numbers of Company X's shares. What are they guilty of? (2 expressions) What should the financial institution do to prevent this?

5 A company selling weapons to a foreign government makes secret payments to politicians who make decisions on which companies to buy arms from. What could these payments be called? (4 expressions) What is the company and the government guilty of? (2 expressions)

40.2 Complete this table, using information from C opposite. The first row has been done for you. You may wish to refer to a dictionary.

Noun: crime	Noun: criminal	Verb: what the criminal does (He/She ...)	Noun: thing made or done in the crime	Related adjective
counterfeiting	counterfeiter	counterfeits	a counterfeit	counterfeit
	embezzler			
	faker	fakes	a	
			a forgery	
fraud	fraudster	defrauds	a	
	money launderer		–	–
		racketeers	–	–

Over to you

Which act of wrongdoing in this unit do you think is the most serious?
Which do you think is the least serious?

Is financial wrongdoing a 'victimless crime'?

41 Ethics

A Code of ethics

Ethics are moral beliefs about what is right and wrong, and the study of this. Some actions are not criminal, but they are morally wrong: **unethical**. Areas where choices have to be made about right and wrong behaviour are **ethical issues**. Some organizations have a **code of ethics** or **code of conduct** where they say what their managers' and employees' behaviour should be, to try to prevent them behaving **unethically**.

B Ethical standards

Ten years ago, Zoe Fleet and Lena Nimble founded FN, which makes trainers (running shoes). Zoe explains:

> We want FN to be **socially responsible** and behave ethically. We don't run plants directly: we buy trainers from plants in Asia. We often visit the plants to check that they don't **exploit** workers by underpaying them or making them work long hours: **sweatshop labor**. In management in the US, we have an **affirmative action program**, to avoid **racial** or **sex discrimination**. (See Unit 8) Every year, we ask an independent expert to do a 'social performance audit' to see how we are doing in these areas. We always publish it, even if we don't like everything in it!

BrE: labour; AmE: labor
BrE: programme; AmE: program

C Ethical investment

Sven Nygren is CEO of the Scandinavian Investment Bank.

'Investors are more and more concerned about where their money is invested. We take **ethical investment** very seriously. We don't invest, for example, in arms companies or tobacco firms. **Environmental** or **green issues** are also very important. Recently we were involved in a project to build a large dam in the Asian country of Paradiso. We discovered that large numbers of farming people would be forced to leave the area flooded by the dam, and that the dam would also be **environmentally damaging**, reducing water supplies to neighbouring countries. It was **green activists** from the environmental organization Green Awareness who told us this. We withdrew from the project and tried to persuade other organizations not to invest in it. We didn't want to damage our reputation for ethical investment.'

41.1 Complete these sentences with words from A opposite.

1 Retailers say packaging that imitates the style and image of market leaders is not wrong and has nothing to do with ....

2 A company is behaving .... if it pollutes the environment.

3 Working conditions are very poor; the organization 'Ethics in Business' blames the .... employers and agencies that exploit the workers.

4 The television industry should adopt a .... on violence in its programmes.

5 '............................ behaviour is good for business,' says Carol Marshall, vice president for ethics and business conduct. 'You get the right kind of employees, and it's a great draw for customers.'

41.2 Complete the crossword with words from A, B and C opposite.

Across

2 Steps taken in the US to avoid discrimination: .... action program. (11)

5 When manual workers are employed in bad conditions with very low pay (BrE). (9,6)

7 When one group of people is unfairly treated differently from another. (14)

10 To pay people badly and make them work in bad conditions (BrE). (7)

11 See 4 down.

13 See 3 down.

Down

1 If your actions do not harm people or the environment, you are socially .... (11)

3, 13 across Putting money into activities that do not harm people or the environment. (7,11)

4, 11 across Topics relating to the environment. (5,6)

6 The world around us. (11)

8 Someone who takes direct action on social or other issues. (8)

9 A written set of rules of behaviour. (4)

Over to you

Do you know of any companies that are famous for their ethical behaviour? Do you choose to buy from them because of this?

What environmental movements are there in your country? What environmental projects are they involved in?

42 Time and time management

A Timeframes and schedules

'**Time is money**,' says the famous phrase. The **timescale** or **timeframe** is the overall period during which something should happen or be completed.
The **lead time** is the period of time it takes to prepare and complete or deliver something.

The times or dates when things should happen is a **schedule** or **timetable**.
If work is completed at the planned time, it is **on schedule**; completion before the planned time is **ahead of schedule** and later is **behind schedule**. If it happens later than planned it is **delayed**; there is **a delay**. If you then try to go faster, you try to **make up time**. But things always **take longer than planned**.

A period when a machine or computer cannot be used because it is not working is **downtime**.

B Projects and project management

A **project** is a carefully planned piece of work to produce something new.

Look at this Gantt chart for building a new supermarket.

Building a new supermarket

		Jun	July	Aug	Sep	Oct	Nov	Dec	Jan	Feb	Mar	Apr	May
stages	Prepare site	✗	✗	✗									
	Build walls			✗	✗	✗							
phases	Build roof						✗	✗	✗				
	Fitting out								✗	✗	✗	✗	
steps	Finish site									✗	✗	✗	
	Recruit employees									✗	✗	✗	
tasks	Opening												✗

These stages **overlap**: the second one starts before the first finishes.

These stages are **simultaneous**; they run **in parallel**. They happen at the same time.

Project management is the managing of these stages. Big projects often include **bonus payments** for **completion** early or **on time**, and **penalties** for late completion.

C Time tips

Lucy Speed runs seminars on how to manage time:

Everyone complains that they never have enough time. Lots of employees do my **time management** courses, to learn how to organize their time. Here are some ideas:

- Use a **diary** (BrE) or **calendar** (AmE) to plan your day and week. **Personal organizers** (small pocket-size computers) are good for this.
- Plan your day **in advance**. Make a **realistic plan** (not just a list) of the things you have to do, in order of importance: **prioritize** them. Work on things that have the highest **priority** first.
- Avoid **interruptions** and **distractions**, which stop you doing what you had planned.
- Do jobs to a realistic level of quality in the time available, and to a level that is really necessary. Don't aim for **perfectionism** when there is no need for it. Try to balance **time**, **cost** and **quality**.

42.1 This is what actually happened in the building of the supermarket described in B opposite. Use appropriate forms of expressions from A and B to complete the text.

	J	J	A	S	O	N	D	J	F	M	A	M	J	J	A	S	O
Prepare site	X	X	X	X	X	X	X										
Build walls								X	X	X							
Build roof											X	X					
Fitting out												X	X	X	X	X	
Finish site													X	X	X		
Recruit employees															X	X	X
Opening																	X

The overall (1) .... was originally 12 months, but the project took 17 months. It started on (2) .... in June, but site preparation took (3) .... because of very bad weather in the autumn. Site preparation and building the walls should have (4) ...., but the walls were started in January. We were able to (5) .... a bit of time on the roof: it took two months instead of three, but we were still behind (6) .... The next (7) .... was fitting out the supermarket, but there was an electricians' strike, so there were (8) .... here too. The store opened in October, but now there's a lot of (9) ...., when the computers don't work.

42.2 Harry is a magazine journalist. Give him advice based on the ideas in C. The first one has been done for you.

1 Harry started the day by making a list of all the things he had to do.
   You should make a realistic plan and prioritize the things you have to do, not just make a list.
2 He started an article, but after five minutes a colleague asked him for help. Harry helped him for half an hour and then they chatted about last night's television.
3 He started on his article again, but he heard police cars outside and went to the window to look.
4 He wanted to make the article look good, so he spent a lot of time adjusting the spacing of the lines, changing the text, etc. even though an editor would do this later.
5 At 6 pm he realised he hadn't started on the other article he had to write, but he went home. On the train, he realized he had arranged to have lunch with an important contact, but had forgotten.
6 Harry decided he needed some training to help him change his behaviour.

Over to you

Do projects usually finish on schedule in your company or country?

How well do you organize your time? What are your secrets of time management?

43 Stress and stress management

A When work is stimulating

'My name's Patricia and I'm a university lecturer. I chose this profession because I wanted to do something **rewarding**: something that gave me satisfaction. Ten years ago, when I started in this job, I had lots to do, but I enjoyed it: preparing and giving lectures, discussing students' work with them and marking it. I felt **stretched**: I had the feeling that work could sometimes be difficult, but that it was **stimulating**, it interested me and made me feel good. It was certainly **challenging**: difficult, but in an interesting and enjoyable way.'

B When stimulation turns to stress

'In the last few years there has been more and more administrative work, with no time for reading or research. I felt **pressure** building up. I began to feel **overwhelmed** by work: I felt as if I wasn't able to do it. I was **under stress**; very worried about my work. I became ill, and I'm sure this was caused by stress: it was **stress-induced**.

Luckily, I was able to deal with the **stresses and strains** (pressures) of my job by starting to work part-time. I was luckier than one of my colleagues, who **became** so **stressed out** because of **overwork** that he had a **nervous breakdown**; he was so worried about work that he couldn't sleep or work, and had to give up. He's completely **burned out**, so stressed and tired by his work that he will never be able to work again. **Burnout** is an increasingly common problem among my colleagues.'

C Downshifting

'Many people want to get away from the **rat race** or the **treadmill**, the feeling that work is too competitive, and are looking for **lifestyles** that are less stressful or completely **unstressful**, a more relaxed ways of living, perhaps in the country. Some people work from home to be near their family and have a better **quality of life**, such as more **quality time** with their children: not just preparing meals for them and taking them to school, etc.

Choosing to live and work in a less stressful way is **downshifting** or **rebalancing**, and people who do this are **downshifters**.'

43.1 Rearrange these sentences containing expressions from A and B opposite.

1 and stimulating. I felt pleasantly stretched. But then the pressure became too much and I felt overworked

2 and under a lot of stress: I found travelling very tiring. I was overwhelmed by my work. I started getting bad headaches, and I'm sure they were stress-induced.

3 challenging to change professions in this way, but now I feel the stress again! I must do something to avoid burning out.

4 Hi, my name's Piet. I'm an engineer, or I was. I worked for a Dutch multinational for 10 years. I was based here in Holland, but my work involved a lot of travelling, visiting factories. At first I liked my job: it was very rewarding

5 So, when I was 35, I made a change. I started a little wine shop in Amsterdam, working on my own. Now, after five years, I have 6 employees. At first it was

43.2 Correct the mistakes in italics with the correct forms of expressions from C opposite.

Shift down a gear to find a sweeter [1]*Lifetype*

YOUR WORK has taken over your life, you are suffering from stress and sick of running to stay in the same place. Solution? Exchange cash for (2) *qualitative time*.

If you feel bored, frustrated and trapped in your job, you are a likely candidate for not just a job change but a 'downshift'. This trend from the US, where it is practised by ten per cent of the working population, has arrived in Britain.

A better word for downshifting would be (3) *reequilibrating*, suggests Judy Jones, co-author of Getting A Life: The Downshifter's Guide to Happier, Simpler Living, a recent guide to a simpler life. 'Trading part of your income for more time is about redefining yourself and your idea of success,' she maintains.

But how do you achieve one aspect of the (4) *downshift's* dream – financial independence? First, try living on less money. Ms Jones suggests you don't use money to keep the (5) *footmill* turning. In her case, she found a third of her income was her '(6) *mouse race* membership fee', spent on work-related activities like eating fast foods, taking holidays to get away from it all and having massages to relieve stress.

Downshifting doesn't necessarily mean changing your job, but taking steps to stop your work taking over your life. It can involve flexible working, job sharing, school term-time working, or cutting down to fewer days at work. All of these things can lead to a better (7) *quantity of live*. ◆

Over to you

Do you sometimes get stressed at work or college? What do you do about it?

Is stress-related illness common in your country?

44 Leadership and management styles

A Leadership

Ken Manners is an expert on leadership and management styles. Can leadership be taught? Or are the only real leaders born leaders?

'Traditionally, the model for **leadership** in business has been the army. Managers and army officers give orders and their **subordinates** (the people working below them) carry them out. Managers, like army officers, may be sent on leadership courses to develop their **leadership skills,** their ability to lead. But they still need a basic **flair** or talent for leadership.'

Leadership

What makes a great leader?

'The greatest leaders have **charisma,** an attractive quality that makes other people admire them and want to follow them. A leader may be described as a **visionary,** someone with the power to see clearly how things are going to be in the future. People often say leaders have **drive, dynamism** and **energy.**'

B Modern management styles

How have management styles changed in the last few years?

'Before, leaders were **distant** and **remote,** not easy to get to know or communicate with. Today, managers are more **open** and **approachable:** you can talk to them easily. There is more management by **consensus,** where decisions are not **imposed** from above in a **top-down approach,** but arrived at by asking employees to contribute in a process of **consultation.**'

Do you think this trend will continue?

'Yes. There are more women managers now, who are often more able to build consensus than traditional military-style **authoritarian** male managers.'

C Empowerment

What, exactly, is empowerment?

'Encouraging employees to use their own **initiative,** to take decisions on their own without asking managers first, is **empowerment. Decision-making** becomes more **decentralized** and less **bureaucratic,** less dependent on managers and systems. This is often necessary where the number of management levels is reduced.

To empower employees, managers need the ability to **delegate,** to give other people responsibility for work rather than doing it all themselves. Of course, with empowerment and **delegation,** the problem is keeping control of your operations: a key issue of modern management.'

44.1 Match the sentence beginnings (1–7) with the correct endings (a–g). The sentences all contain words from A opposite.

1 We are looking for a new CEO, someone with strong leadership
2 Richard has real managerial flair
3 In the police, leaders are held responsible
4 The study concludes that a charismatic visionary leader is absolutely not required for a visionary company
5 She is an extraordinary leader
6 Thatcher had drive, energy and vision,
7 He was a born leader. When everyone else was discussing

a but many thought it was the wrong vision.
b and, in fact, can be bad for a company's long-term prospects.
c and has won the respect of colleagues and employees.
d for the actions of their subordinates.
e skills and experience with financial institutions.
f what to do, he knew exactly what to do.
g who will bring dynamism and energy to the job.

44.2 Complete the crossword with the correct forms of words from B and C opposite.

Across

1, 7 down What managers do, with or without talking to employees. (8,6)
5 Adjective to describe leading without consultation. (13)
8 Not easy to talk to. (7)
9 See 13 across.
11 What the type of boss in 5 across does not do. (7)
13, 9 Managers deciding without talking to employees is a .... - down ....(3,8)
14 If managers ask employees to take on responsibility, they .... (8)
15 If all the decisions are not made in a company's head office, it is .... (13)

Down

2 To allow employees to decide things for themselves. (7)
3 An organization where there are a lot of rules and procedures is .... (12)
4 If you decide without asking a manager, you use .... (10)
6 The adjective relating to 'consensus'. (10)
7 See 1 across.
10 If decisions are not arrived at by consensus, they are .... (7)
12 Easy to see and talk to. (4)

Over to you

What are the characteristics of a true leader? Do you think you have the qualities of a good manager/leader? Would you be authoritarian or approachable?

45 Business across cultures 1

A · Cultures and culture

Alexandra Adler is an expert in doing business across cultures. She is talking to a group of British businesspeople.

'**Culture** is the "way we do things here". "Here" may be a country, an area, a social class or an organization such as a company or school. You often talk about:

- **company** or **corporate culture**: the way a particular company works, and the things it believes are important.
- **canteen culture**: the ways that people in an organization such as the police think and talk, not approved by the leaders of the organization.
- **long-hours culture**: where people are expected to work for a long time each day.
- **macho culture**: ideas typically associated with men: physical strength, aggressiveness, etc.

But you must be careful of **stereotypes**, fixed ideas that may not be true.'

B · Distance and familiarity

Distance between managers and the people who work under them varies in different cultures. (See Unit 44) Look at these two companies.

In Country A, managers are usually easy to talk to – **accessible** and **approachable** – and there is a tradition of employees being involved in **decision-making** as part of a **team of equals**.	In Country B, managers are usually more **distant** and **remote**. Employees may feel quite distant from their managers and have a lot of **deference** for them: accepting decisions but not participating in them.

Call me Stefan.

Call me Mr Johnson.

This company is not very **hierarchical**, with only three **management layers**. (See Unit 9)	Companies in Country B tend to be more **hierarchical** than those in Country A, with more **management layers**.

Deference and distance may be shown in language. Some languages have many **forms of address** that you use to indicate how **familiar** you are with someone. English only has one form, 'you', but distance may be shown in other ways, for example, in whether first names or surnames are used. (See Unit 46)

45.1 Look at A opposite. Which word combination with 'culture' describes each of the following?

1 The men really dominate in this company, they don't make life easy for women at all. All they talk about is football.
2 Among the management here we try to be fair to people from different minorities, but there are still elements of racism among the workforce.
3 Of course, the quality of the work you do after you've been at it for ten hours is not good.
4 There was a time when managers could only wear white shirts in this company – things are a bit less formal now.
5 Here the male managers talk about the market as if it was some kind of battlefield.
6 They say that if you go home at 5.30, you can't be doing your job properly, but I'm going anyway.

45.2 Read this information about two very different companies and answer the questions.

The Associated Box Company (ABC) and the Superior Box Corporation (SBC) both make cardboard boxes.

At ABC there are three levels of management between the CEO and the people who actually make the boxes. At SBC, there is only one level.

Managers at ABC are very distant. They rarely leave their offices, they have their own executive restaurant and the employees hardly ever see them. Employees are never consulted in decision-making. At SBC, managers share the same canteen with employees. Managers have long meetings with employees before taking important decisions.

Managers and the CEO of SBC have an open-door policy where employees can come to see them about any complaint they might have. At ABC, employees must sort out problems with the manager immediately above them.

At ABC, employees call their managers 'sir'. At SBC, everyone uses first names.

1 Which company:
  a is more hierarchical?
  b is more informal in the way people talk to each other?

2 In which company are managers:
  a more approachable?
  b more remote?

3 In which company are employees:
  a more deferential?
  b on more equal terms with their bosses?

Over to you

Is your organization more like ABC or SBC above? Which type of company would you prefer to work for? What are the advantages and disadvantages of each type of company?

46 Business across cultures 2

A Names

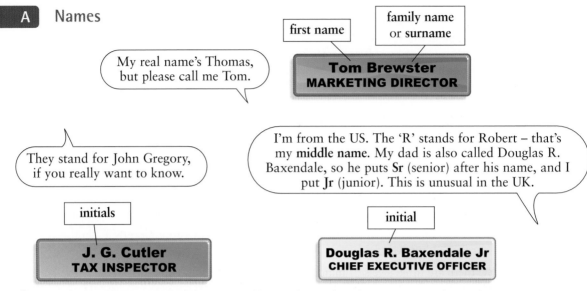

first name

family name or surname

My real name's Thomas, but please call me Tom.

Tom Brewster
MARKETING DIRECTOR

I'm from the US. The 'R' stands for Robert – that's my **middle name**. My dad is also called Douglas R. Baxendale, so he puts **Sr** (senior) after his name, and I put **Jr** (junior). This is unusual in the UK.

They stand for John Gregory, if you really want to know.

initials

initial

J. G. Cutler
TAX INSPECTOR

Douglas R. Baxendale Jr
CHIEF EXECUTIVE OFFICER

⚠️ In the English-speaking business world, people use first names, even with people they do not know very well. But if you aren't sure, use **Mr** and the family name for men, and **Mrs** or **Miss** and the family name for women, depending on whether they are married or not. **Ms** often replaces Mrs and Miss. You don't use Mr, Mrs, Miss or Ms with only a first name (e.g. ~~Mr John~~) or by itself.

B Business cards

qualifications

Megabook **Publishing**

34 Dean Street, Soho, London W1R 4EF

job title

JAMES CASSIDY
Sales Director

Tel: 020 7452 8960
Fax: 020 7452 8965
E-mail james.cassidy@megabook.com

Abrahams, Campbell, Esposito
Corporate Accountants

7590 W Charleston Blvd
Las Vegas, NV 89147
(702) 258-9783

KAREN A. ESPOSITO, B.S., C.P.A.
Senior Partner
e-mail: kesposito@ace.com

C Dress

In Alphaland, businesspeople dress quite **formally**. The **business suit** is common, but for men, wearing non-matching jacket and trousers is also a possibility.

In Betatania, the dark **business suit** is obligatory for men. Some companies allow women to wear trouser suits.

In Gammaria, the business suit is almost as necessary as in Betatania, but with more variation in colours. Some companies require employees to wear formal clothes from Monday to Thursday, and allow less formal ones on what they call **casual Fridays** or **dress-down Fridays**. In some places, many banks and shops require people dealing with customers to wear **uniforms** so that they all dress the same.

In Deltatonia, people dress more **casually** at work than in the other countries. For men, suits and ties are less common than elsewhere. This is **smart casual**.

46.1 Look at A opposite and decide whether these pieces of advice about the English-speaking business world are true or false.

1 It's possible to introduce yourself by saying your family name then your first name.
2 It's possible to use Mr, Mrs or Miss on its own, or with a first name.
3 British people use Sr and Jr to refer to a father and his son.
4 Americans often show their middle name with an initial.
5 You can always use someone's first name to talk to them, even if you don't know them very well.
6 Ms is being used more and more as a title for women.
7 You can show your qualifications after your name on your business card.

46.2 Which country in C opposite does each of these people come from?

1 ....

2 ....

3 ....

4 ....

Over to you

How are names used in business in your country?

How do people dress at work? Do any companies have dress-down days in your country? What are the advantages and disadvantages of how people dress?

A Entertainment and hospitality

Alexandra Adler continues her seminar on cross-cultural issues.

Entertaining and **hospitality** vary a lot in different cultures.

- In Alphaland, entertaining is important. There are long **business lunches** in restaurants, where deals are discussed. Professional and private life are separate, and clients are never invited home.
- In Betatania, evenings are spent drinking and singing in bars with colleagues and clients.
- In Gammaria, lunch can be important, but less so than in Alphaland. Important contacts may be invited to dinner at home. **Corporate hospitality** is a big industry, with clients invited to big sports events.
- In Deltatonia, restaurants are rare outside the capital. Some entertainment takes place when important clients are invited to people's houses for dinner, or go sailing or to country houses for the weekend, etc.

B Time

Attitudes towards time can vary enormously.

In Busyville, people start work at eight, and officially finish at six, though many managers stay much longer. There is a culture of **presenteeism**: being at work when you don't need to be.

There is a two-hour **lunch break**, and a lot of business is done over restaurant lunches. (Lunch is the main meal. The **working breakfast** is rare.) There are no snacks between meals, just coffee, so eat properly at meal times.

As for **punctuality**, you can arrive up to 15 minutes 'late' for meetings. If invited to someone's house (unusual in business), arrive 15–30 minutes after the time given.

Don't phone people at home about work, and don't phone them at all after 9 pm.

There are a lot of **public holidays** (about 15) during the year. Busyville is empty in August, as many companies close completely for four weeks. Employees have five weeks' **holiday** a year and they usually take four of them in August.

> BrE: holiday
> AmE: vacation

C Cross-cultural communication

Here are some other areas of potential cultural misunderstanding:

a **distance when talking to people**: what is comfortable?
b **eye contact**: how much of the time do people look directly at each other?
c **gesture**: do people make lots of facial gestures? How much do they move their arms and hands?
d **greetings/goodbyes**: do people shake hands every time? Are there fixed phrases to say?
e **humour**: is this a good way of relaxing people? Or is it out of place in some contexts?
f **physical contact**: how much do people touch each other?
g **presents**: when should you give them? When should you open them? What should you say when you receive one?
h **rules of conversation and the role of silence**: how long can people be silent before they feel uncomfortable? Is it acceptable to interrupt when others are speaking?

> BrE: humou
> AmE: humo

47.1 In which country from A opposite might you hear these things?

1 How about a trip out tomorrow afternoon? We could see some horse racing and have a glass of champagne.
2 Do come out with us this evening! I know some great bars. How's your singing?
3 What are you doing this weekend? You could come to our summer cottage. You'll meet my family and we can take the boat out.
4 Let's get out of the office to discuss the deal. I know a nice restaurant near here, with some very good local dishes.

47.2 Look at B opposite. Tick (✔) the things this visitor to Busyville does right, and put a cross (✗) by her mistakes.

I phoned my contact in her office at 7.30 pm. (1...) I suggested a working breakfast the next morning. (2...) She wasn't keen, so I suggested lunch. (3...) We arranged to meet at her office at 12.30. I arrived at 12.45 (4...) and we went to a restaurant, where we had a very good discussion. That evening I wanted to check something, so I found her name in the phone book and phoned her at home. (5...) She was less friendly than at lunchtime. I said I would be back in Busyville in mid-August (6...). Not a good time, she said, so I suggested September. (7...)

47.3 Which points in C opposite are referred to in this story?

Sally, a student, is working for a company abroad for work experience. The company has employees from all over the world. The head of the company, Henrik, invites Sally to a barbecue for his employees at his home, at 3 pm on Saturday.

She is the first to arrive, at exactly 3 o'clock. When the others arrive, some shake hands with each other. Some kiss on one cheek, others on both cheeks. Others arrive and say hello without kissing or shaking hands. (1...) Some bring wine or flowers, which the host does not open and puts to one side. Others bring nothing. (2...)

In conversations, some people move their arms around a lot and seem to make signs with their hands, others keep their hands by their sides. (3...) Some people do not let others finish what they are saying, and others say almost nothing; the people with them seem upset and move away when they can. (4...) Some people look directly at the person they are talking to. Others look away more. (5...) Some touch the arm of the other person whenever they are speaking to them. (6...) She notices that some people seem to be slowly moving backwards across the garden as the conversation goes on, while the person with them is moving forward. (7...)

Later, somebody makes a joke but nobody laughs. Everyone goes quiet. (8...) People start saying goodbye and leaving.

Over to you

What should visitors to your country know about the points in A, B and C opposite?

48 Telephoning 1: phones and numbers

A Telephones and beyond

- **public telephone** / **payphone**: phone in a public place operated with money, a credit card or a **phone card**.
- **mobile phone, mobile** (BrE) / **cellphone, cellular phone, cellular** (AmE): a phone you can take with you and use anywhere.
- **WAP phone**: a mobile phone with access to the Internet (WAP = wireless application protocol).
- **extension**: one of a number of phones on the same **line**, in a home or office.
- **cordless phone, cordless**: an extension not connected by a wire, so you can use it around the house or in the garden.
- **pager**: allows you to receive written messages
- **webcam**: a camera attached to a computer and phone line, so two people talking on the phone can see each other.
- **videophone**: a special phone with a screen so you can see the other person.

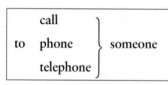

Webcams and videophones enable **videoconferencing**: holding a meeting with people in different locations.

B Phone, call and ring

to	call phone telephone	} someone

to give someone a call

BrE: to ring someone, to ring up someone, to ring someone up, to give someone a ring

Informal BrE: to give someone a bell, to give someone a buzz

AmE: to call someone, to call up someone, to call someone up

C Numbers

When saying numbers, use rising intonation for each group, except for the last group, when you should use a falling tone. This shows you have reached the end of the number.

access code	country code	area code	number
00 ↗	44 ↗	1746 ↗	845 921 ↗ ↘
Double oh (BrE) Zero zero (AmE)	double four	one seven four six	eight four five nine two one

D Doing things over the phone

Phone numbers where you can get information or advice, buy things, make reservations, etc. may be called:

- **helpline**
- **hotline**
- **information line**
- **reservations line**

People who answer and deal with calls like these work in **call centres** (AmE: **call centers**).

A number that is free of charge is:

BrE	AmE
■ an **0800 number*** ■ a **Freephone number**	■ a **1-800 number** ■ a **toll-free number**

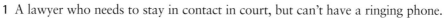

48.1 Which equipment in A opposite would each of these people use?

1 A lawyer who needs to stay in contact in court, but can't have a ringing phone.
2 A building contractor who works in different places.
3 Someone who wants to stay in touch whilst they are in the garden.
4 A company manager who wants to discuss something with managers in different offices at the same time.
5 A computer enthusiast who wants to see the person she is talking to.
6 Someone who is out but doesn't have a mobile.

48.2 Which of these sentences containing expressions from B opposite are correct? Correct the mistakes.

1 It would be good to see Anna soon. I'll phone to her and see when she's free.
2 I gave Brian a call yesterday and we had a long chat.
3 Why don't you ring up at Pizza Palace and order some takeaway pizza?
4 I rung them five minutes ago but there was no answer.
5 Call me up next time you're in New York.
6 Give me a ring when you're next in London.
7 I'll give her the bell and we'll fix up a meeting.
8 When you get some news, make me a buzz.

48.3 Write out these numbers in words (use American English).
Show the intonation with arrows, as in C opposite.
The first one has been done for you.

1 Empire State Building, New York 212-736 3100.

Two-one-two seven-three-six three-one-zero-zero

2 Disney World, Orlando, Florida 407-824 4321
3 Paramount Studios, Hollywood 213-956 1777
4 Alamo, San Antonio, Texas 210-225 1391
5 Graceland, Memphis, Tennessee 901-332 3322
6 Grand Canyon, Colorado 520-638 2626

48.4 Match what the people say below with words from D opposite.

1 Just call this number to book your seats.

2 For technical assistance with your new computer, call ...

3 If you know the answer call us right here in the studio! Right now!

4 Call us any time to find out about opening times and admission prices.

5 To buy this amazing product, simply call 0800 ...

Over to you

When was the last time you called an organization for information? What happened?

Do you like recorded information, or do you prefer to talk to a real person?

Does your organization (or one you are interested in) offer recorded information?

49 Telephoning 2: getting through

A Phoning scenario

You want to phone someone in a company. You pick up the phone. You hear the **dialling tone** and **dial** the number on the **keypad**. You don't know the person's **direct line** number, so you **dial** the number of the company's **switchboard**. One of these things happens:

a The number rings but no one answers.

b You hear the **engaged tone** (BrE) / **busy tone** (AmE) because the other person is already talking on the phone. You **hang up** and try again later.

c You **get through**, but not to the number you wanted. The person who answers says you've got the **wrong number**.

d The **operator** answers. You ask for the **extension** of the person you want to speak to.

e You are **put through** to the wrong extension. The person offers to **transfer** you to the right extension, but you are **cut off** – the call ends.

f The person you want to speak to is not at their desk and you leave a message on their **voicemail**. You ask them to **call you back** or to **return your call**.

B Asking to speak to someone 1

> Can you put me through to extension 123, please?
> Can I have extension 123, please?
> Extension 123, please.
> 123, please.
> James Cassidy in Sales, please.

> One moment, please.
> I'm putting you through.
> The extension/line is ringing for you.

> Sorry to keep you waiting.

> I think you've got the wrong extension.
> I'll try and transfer you.

> I phoned a moment ago, but I was cut off.

> I'm afraid the line's/extension's busy/engaged.
> I'm sorry, but there's no reply

> I'll { hold. call back later.

> Do you want to hold or would you like to call back later?

C Voicemail

If the person you want to speak to is not there, you may hear this:

> You're through to the voicemail of James Cassidy. I'm not at my desk right now, but if you leave a message, I'll get right back to you. To leave a message, press 1. To speak to the operator, please hold.

After you leave your message, you may hear this:

> To listen to your message, press 2.

After you listen to your message, you may hear this:

> If you'd like to change your message, press 3. If you'd like to erase your message, press 4. Otherwise, please hang up.

49.1 You are trying to phone Delia Jones. She works in a large company. Match your possible reactions (1–7) to the things (a–f) described in A opposite. One of the things is used twice.

1 That's strange. Their switchboard isn't big enough to handle all the calls they get.
2 That's ridiculous! A company with 500 employees, but no one answers the phone.
3 I ask for Delia Jones and they put me through to Della Jones!
4 Delia seems to spend all day on the phone. Her line's always busy.
5 That's strange. I'm sure I dialled the right number.
6 Oh no I hate this – oh well, I'd better leave a message ...
7 They never seem able to find the extension number!

49.2 Look at B opposite. Annelise Schmidt is trying to phone James Cassidy. Put the conversation into a logical order.

1 Annelise: Good morning. Can I speak to James Cassidy in Sales?
2 Annelise: Is that James Cassidy?
3 Annelise: No, I'm afraid I don't.
4 Annelise: Thanks. Oh no, I've been cut off.
5 Switchboard operator: Do you know the extension?
6 Switchboard operator: Sorry to keep you waiting. ... I'm putting you through.
7 John Cassidy: Cassidy.
8 John Cassidy: No, this is John Cassidy. You've come through to Accounts. I'll try and transfer you back to the switchboard.

49.3 Look at Unit 48 and the opposite page. Correct the nine mistakes in Annelise Schmidt's voicemail message.

Hi James, this is Annelise calling out of Sprenger Verlag in Hamburg. It's very difficult to get hold to you. I phoned to you earlier, but your telephone central placed me through to the bad telephone. Anyway, I'm calling to you to discuss the contract we were talking about in Frankfurt. I'll call further later or perhaps you'd like to ring to me here in Hamburg on 00 49 40 789 1357. Bye for now.

Over to you

Have you ever had these problems on the phone, in your language or in English?

Do you use voicemail yourself? What are its advantages and disadvantages?

50 Telephoning 3: messages

A Asking to speak to someone 2

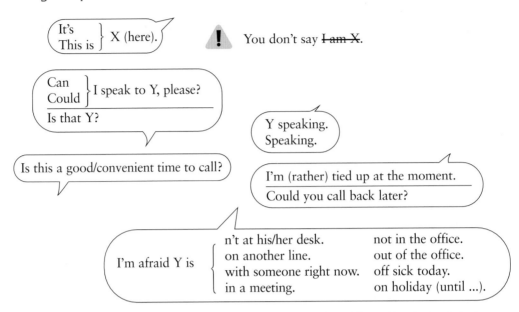

It's / This is } X (here).

⚠ You don't say ~~I am X.~~

Can / Could } I speak to Y, please?
___
Is that Y?

Y speaking.
Speaking.

Is this a good/convenient time to call?

I'm (rather) tied up at the moment.
___
Could you call back later?

I'm afraid Y is
- n't at his/her desk.
- on another line.
- with someone right now.
- in a meeting.
- not in the office.
- out of the office.
- off sick today.
- on holiday (until ...).

B Giving and taking messages

I'm calling about ...
___
I'm calling to confirm that ...
___
Could I leave a message?
___
Could you tell Y that ...?
___
Could you ask Y to call me back? My number's ...

I wonder if you could call back later?
___
Can I ask who's calling?
Who's calling please?
___
Which company are you calling from?
___
May/Can I ask what it's about?
___
May/Can I take a message?
Would you like to leave a message?

I'll ask him/her to call you (when he/she gets back).

C Spelling names

If you want to spell a name, you can say, for example, 'A for Alpha', 'B as in Bravo', etc.

You may also need these expressions:

- ■ capital A
- ■ small a
- ■ all one word
- ■ new word/line
- ■ dash or hyphen (-)
- ■ slash (/)
- ■ dot (.)
- ■ at (@)

D Taking messages: checking information

a I'm sorry, I didn't catch your name. Could you spell it, please?

b Is that with a D at the end, D for David?

c Did you say your number is 624 426?

d Is that with B for Bravo or V for Victor?

e Where did you say you're calling from?

f Is that with one M in the middle or two?

g The code for Sweden is 49, right?

h Is that Ginola like the football player?

50.1 Look at A and B opposite and change these conversations so that they are correct and more polite.

1

A: I want to speak to Mrs Lee.
B: That's me but I'm busy.
A: Sven Nyman talking. I want to talk about your order.
B: Call me back later.

2

A: Are you James Cassidy?
B: No. Who are you?
A: Annelise Schmidt. Is James Cassidy there and, if he is, can I speak to him?
B: He can't speak to you. He's in a meeting. Give me a message.
A: He has to call me as soon as possible.

50.2 Spell the following as you would spell them on the phone. Use the table below to help you. The first one has been done for you.

Alpha	Bravo	Charlie	Delta	Echo	Foxtrot
Golf	Hotel	India	Juliet	Kilo	Lima
Mike	November	Oscar	Papa	Quebec	Romeo
Sierra	Tango	Uniform	Victor	Whisky	X-ray
Yankee	Zulu				

1 Maeght: M for Mike, A for Alpha, E for Echo, G for Golf, H for Hotel, T for Tango.

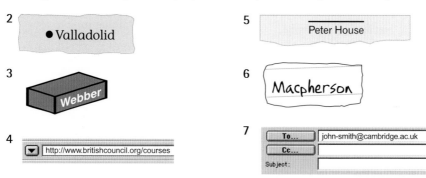

2 •Valladolid

3 Webber

4 http://www.britishcouncil.org/courses

5 Peter House

6 Macpherson

7 To... john-smith@cambridge.ac.uk
   Cc...
   Subject:

50.3 Match the responses (1–8) with the questions (a–h) in D opposite.

1 No, actually it's 46.
2 It's Valladolid with a V at the beginning, V for Victor.
3 No, it's Schmidt with a T at the end, T for Tommy.
4 Two. T-I-double-M-E-R-M-A-N.
5 No, 642 246.
6 Springer Verlag in Hamburg.
7 Krieslovski. K-R-I-E-S-L-O-V-S-K-I.
8 No, it's with two Ns in the middle.

Over to you

What is the most difficult thing when you phone someone in another language?

Practise words you often have to spell on the phone, using the alphabet above.

51 Telephoning 4: arrangements

A Making arrangements

You get through to the person you want to speak to and fix a meeting.

> Can/Shall we fix/arrange an appointment/a meeting?
> Would it be useful to meet up soon?

> I'll (just) get / check my diary

> How about Monday?
> What about Tuesday?
> Would Wednesday be suitable?
> Would Thursday suit you?
> Shall we say Friday?

> That's fine.
> I can't / won't be able to make Monday.
> I've got to (+ infinitive) / a (+ noun) ...

B Closing the conversation

Here are some ways of finishing a conversation without sounding abrupt (rude).

See you on Friday then.

I'm going to have to go now.

I've got to {
go to a meeting.
go and see someone.
}

(It's been) nice talking to you.

Good to talk to you.

Talk to you soon, no doubt.

We'll be (back) in touch soon.

Look forward to hearing from you soon.

Yes, I'll look forward to seeing you on Friday.

Nice talking to you.

(It's been) good talking to you.

Thanks for {
calling.
phoning.
}

C Changing arrangements

Here are some ways of changing arrangements.

a I **can't make** Tuesday (Tuesday is not possible). **Something has come up** (has occurred to prevent our meeting). **I've got to** go over to Berlin to see a client. **How about** Wednesday?

b I think we said Thursday at 11. **Can you make** the afternoon instead? (Is it possible for you to meet in the afternoon?)

c We're going to have to change our arrangement for the 15th. Can we **put it off** (delay it) till the 22nd? I'd completely forgotten we have a departmental meeting that day.

d I'm afraid Monday **won't be possible** after all. I'm going to be very busy that day. What about the following week?

e We're going to have to **put back** (delay) our meeting. **I'm completely snowed under** (very busy) at the moment. **Can we leave it open** (decide not to fix a day) for the time being? **I'll get back in touch** (contact you again) when I'm not so busy.

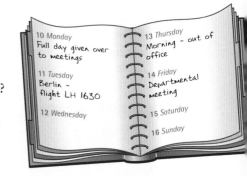

10 Monday
Full day given over to meetings

11 Tuesday
Berlin – flight LH 1630

12 Wednesday

13 Thursday
Morning – out of office

14 Friday
Departmental meeting

15 Saturday

16 Sunday

51.1 Annelise Schmidt (AS) gets through to James Cassidy (JC) and arranges to meet him. Reorder their conversation, which contains expressions from A and B opposite.

  a AS: Fine thanks. I'm going to be in London on Tuesday and Wednesday next week. How about meeting up to discuss how Megabook and Sprenger might work together?

  b AS: Hello. This is Annelise Schmidt. You remember we met at the Frankfurt Book Fair last month?

  c AS: Look forward to seeing you then. Bye.

  d AS: Sounds good. Shall I meet you at your office? I've got the address.

  e AS: Yes, that's fine.

  f JC: James Cassidy.

  g JC: Goodbye.

  h JC: I'll just check my diary. I won't be able to make Tuesday. I've got to go to Manchester. Would Wednesday suit you? How about lunch?

  i JC: OK. See you on Wednesday at 12.30, then.

  j JC: Yes, how are you?

  k JC: Yes. Why don't you come round here at about 12.30? Ask for me at reception and I'll come down.

51.2 Look at B opposite. Which of these conversations sound natural, and which sound strange?

  1 A: Nice talking to you. See you on Wednesday.
     B: See you Wednesday. Thanks for calling. Bye.
  2 A: I'll look forward to seeing you tomorrow, then.
     B: Talk to you soon, no doubt. Bye.
  3 A: It's been good talking to you. I'm going to have to go. I've got to go to a meeting.
     B: Nice talking to you. I'll be in touch soon.
  4 A: See you this afternoon at four, then.
     B: Yes, we'll be back in touch soon.
  5 A: I'm going to have to go.
     B: OK. Talk to you soon, no doubt. Bye.

51.3 Match these replies (1–5) to the things (a–e) the people say in C opposite.

  1 I suppose so: it would have been good to meet. Look forward to hearing from you when you're less busy.
  2 The 22nd ... I'm going to be on holiday. What about the 29th?
  3 The afternoon would be no problem. How about at three?
  4 Wednesday's going to be difficult. Can you make the next day?
  5 Yes, the same day the following week would be fine.

Over to you

Do you make arrangements on the phone?

Do you find it difficult to end phone calls?

52 Faxes

A Sending faxes

Jaime Vasconcelos in Los Angeles, USA is on the phone
to Anna Friedman in Sydney, Australia.

Anna: Yes, I think you'll be interested in our latest designs.
Jaime: Can you **send them by fax**?   to send something by fax
Anna: Sure. **I'll fax you** right now. What's your **fax number**?   to fax someone
Jaime: 1 for the US, then 213 976 3421.
Anna: OK. I've got that.
Jaime: Can you **fax the information** you think we need?   to fax something
Anna: I'll **fax you everything we have**. There are about 30 pages.   to fax someone something
Jaime: If you could **fax it all over to us**, that would be great!   to fax something (over/across) to someone

B Fax layout

1 **cover sheet**: the first page of a fax showing who it's from, who it's to, etc.

2 **confidential information**: things that others should not know

3 **intended recipient**: the person who should receive the fax

4 **advise the sender**: tell the person who sent it

ADVANCED ENGINEERING

FAX COVER SHEET[1]

Box 1212, Sydney, Australia
Tel: 61 2 329 9220
Fax: 61 2 329 9221

Date: 22 November   To fax number: +1 213 976 3421

To: Jaime Vasconcelos   From: Anna Friedman

Number of pages including this cover sheet: 31

Dear Jaime,

It was good to hear from you again. The following pages give details of the latest additions to our range. If you require any further information, please do not hesitate to contact me.

Best regards,

Anna Friedman

This fax may contain confidential information[2]. If you are not the intended recipient[3], advise the sender[4] and destroy this document.

If you do not receive all pages, or if any pages are illegible,

please phone +61 2 329 9220 immediately.

«22/11/01→⊙11:30:42» FROM: 61 2 329 9221 TO: + 213 976 3421

C Receiving faxes

Anna: Did you **get my fax**?
Jaime: You're not going to believe this, but **the paper got stuck** and the **machine jammed**.
Anna: No problem. I'll **send** it **through** again.

15 minutes later ...

Anna: Did the fax **go through** OK this time?
Jaime: Yes, but pages two and three weren't **legible**: I couldn't read them.
Anna: No problem. I'll **resend** them.

52.1 Bertil Lagerkvist of Moda Fashions in Stockholm is talking to Kim Wang of Outrageous Designs in Hong Kong. Look at A opposite and correct the mistakes.

K: Yes, I think you'll be interested.
B: Can you (1) telefax your most exciting designs?
K: Sure, I'll (2) fax to you the drawings. What's your (3) number of fax?
B: 46 for Sweden, then 8 753 4298.
K: 46 8 753 4298. I've got that.
B: You know the sort of thing we sell. Can you (4) telefax to me the designs our customers will be most interested in?
K: I'll (5) fax to you straightaway. There are about ten pages.
B: If you could fax everything (6) between, that would be great!

52.2 Kim Wang sends a fax to Stockholm. The person receiving the fax phones Kim. Read what is said, and complete the statements using expressions from B opposite.

1 'Swedish Paper Products here. We've received a fax from you to a company called Moda Fashions. Our fax numbers are very similar. There must be some mistake.'

Swedish Paper Products (SPP) are not the ...., and so they tell the person sending the fax: they .... the ....

2 'The designs you received are top secret. Please could you tear them up and throw them away.'

The information is .... Kim wants SPP to .... the fax so that no one else can see it.

3 'Don't worry. There's something wrong with our fax machine so we can't read it anyway, including most of the first page.'

The person can't read the fax: the fax, including most of the .... is ....

52.3 Kim Wang sends the fax again, this time to the correct number. Complete the commentary, choosing appropriate forms of the expressions in brackets from B and C opposite.

There were no problems when she .... (1 send again / resend) the fax. The fax .... (2 send through / go through) perfectly: the paper .... (3 not get stuck / not get through) and the machine .... (4 legible/jam). Kim did not have to .... anything .... (5 go through / send through) again. The fax was .... (6 legible/stuck) and Bertil could read it.

Over to you

Do you send and receive many faxes or do you rely mainly on email?
What are faxes particularly useful for?

53 Emails

A Email

Email is **electronic mail.** You can **send an email** to someone, or **email** them.
They will **reply** to your email or **email you back.**

reply to all: send an answer to the person who sent an email, and everyone who received a copy of it

reply: send an answer to the person who sent an email

delete: get rid of an email you don't want

cc: send a copy to ...

bcc: send a blind copy to ... (the other people don't know you're sending this copy)

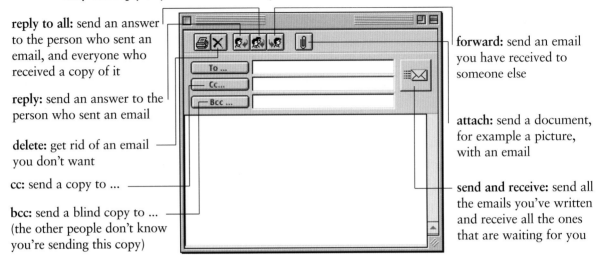

forward: send an email you have received to someone else

attach: send a document, for example a picture, with an email

send and receive: send all the emails you've written and receive all the ones that are waiting for you

B Email expressions

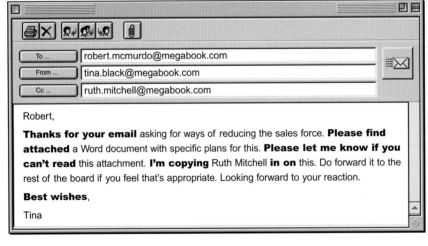

To ... robert.mcmurdo@megabook.com
From ... tina.black@megabook.com
Cc ... ruth.mitchell@megabook.com

Robert,

Thanks for your email asking for ways of reducing the sales force. **Please find attached** a Word document with specific plans for this. **Please let me know if you can't read** this attachment. **I'm copying** Ruth Mitchell **in on** this. Do forward it to the rest of the board if you feel that's appropriate. Looking forward to your reaction.

Best wishes,

Tina

You can end with:

- **Best wishes**
- **All best wishes**
- **Regards**
- **Best regards**

To people you know well, you can end with:

- **All the best**

or even just:

- **Best**

C Email abbreviations

These **abbreviations** are sometimes used in emails

1 As far as I know.
2 Hope this helps.

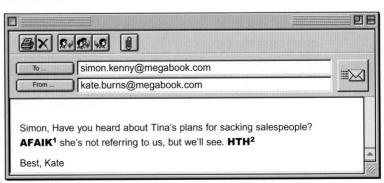

To ... simon.kenny@megabook.com
From ... kate.burns@megabook.com

Simon, Have you heard about Tina's plans for sacking salespeople?
AFAIK[1] she's not referring to us, but we'll see. **HTH**[2]

Best, Kate

53.1 Which of the features in A opposite would you use in each of these situations?

   1 You are sending an email to Antonio and you want to send a copy to Bella without Antonio knowing.
   2 You receive a reply from Antonio, and you want Carlos to see it.
   3 You get an email from Delia, who has also sent copies to Edgar and Fenella, and you want to send the same answer to all three of them.
   4 With the email to Giorgio, you want to send another document.
   5 You've written three emails. You want to send them, and read any that are waiting for you.
   6 You receive two emails, but you don't want to keep them.

53.2 Complete this email using the correct form of expressions from B that mean the same as the underlined expressions.

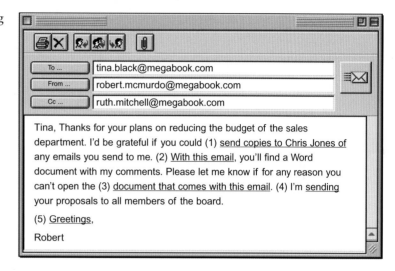

Tina, Thanks for your plans on reducing the budget of the sales department. I'd be grateful if you could (1) <u>send copies to Chris Jones of</u> any emails you send to me. (2) <u>With this email</u>, you'll find a Word document with my comments. Please let me know if for any reason you can't open the (3) <u>document that comes with this email</u>. (4) I'm <u>sending</u> your proposals to all members of the board.

(5) <u>Greetings,</u>

Robert

53.3 Complete the extracts from these emails, using the abbreviations from C opposite.

1
I'm not sure about this, but .... there seems to be a reorganization going on in the company.

2
You asked about sales figures for three years ago. Please see the attached document. .... Good luck preparing next year's budget!

Over to you

What do you use email for? Does email save time, or does it just make more work?
Should employees send and receive personal emails at work?

54 Meetings 1: types of meeting

Word combinations with 'meeting'

arrange set up fix		organize a meeting
bring forward		make a meeting earlier than originally decided
put back postpone	a meeting	make a meeting later than originally planned
cancel		not have a meeting after all
run chair		be in charge of a meeting
attend		go to a meeting
miss		not go to a meeting

B Types of meeting

Meetings come in all shapes and sizes, of course. Here are some types:

■ **chat** (informal discussion) with colleagues at the coffee machine.
■ **brainstorming** among colleagues: where as many ideas as possible are produced quickly, to be evaluated later.
■ **project meeting / team meeting** of employees involved in a particular activity.
■ **department/departmental meeting**.
■ **meeting with suppliers**, for example to negotiate prices for an order.
■ **meeting with a customer**, for example to discuss a contract.
■ **board meeting**: an official, formal meeting of a company's directors.
■ **Annual general meeting / AGM** (BrE); **annual meeting** (AmE): where shareholders discuss the company's annual report.
■ **EGM**: extraordinary general meeting: a shareholders' meeting to discuss an important issue such as a proposed merger.

C How was the meeting?

Some colleagues are discussing a meeting they have just come out of.

Anil: I thought it was very **productive**.
Juliet: Well, I thought it was a complete **waste of time**. I didn't hear anything I didn't already know.
Barbara: I agree with Anil. I felt we had some very **useful discussions**, and that we reached an agreement that was good for both sides. We certainly **covered a lot of ground**. It was incredible the number of things we got through.
Juliet: But there were too many **digressions**. John was **rambling** and kept **wandering off the point**. He just uses meetings as a chance to show off. Just like a lot of men: he just wanted to show how powerful he is and what a good talker he is.
Anil: But to be fair, the chair really **kept things moving**: she encouraged people to be brief and to **stick to the point** and we achieved a lot in a short time. Anyway, I learned a lot and I think they listened to what we had to say.

54.1 Replace the underlined expressions with appropriate forms of the verbs in A opposite. In some cases, more than one verb is possible.

A meeting of the Tennis Club Committee was (1) <u>organized</u> for 1 March, but not everyone could (2) <u>go to it</u>, so it was (3) <u>delayed</u> until March 31. One committee member said that this was too late, so eventually we (4) <u>moved it</u> to March 15. The chairperson (5) <u>was in charge of</u> it very efficiently, and we decided on some new membership rules. Only one committee member (6) <u>did not go to</u> the meeting.

54.2 Look at B opposite. At which type of meeting would you be most likely to hear each of these things?

1 I'm pleased to announce another good year for shareholders of this company.
2 I know this sounds crazy, but how about giving away 100,000 free samples?
3 Things in the sales department are getting out of control. We should all start making a real effort.
4 So, you think you can provide 10,000 a month at a unit cost of £4.90?
5 Have you heard? Suzanne is being fired: apparently her sales figures aren't good enough.
6 That's a deal then. Looking forward to working with you. I'm sure you won't be disappointed.
7 Amazingly, we're ahead of schedule on this project.
8 I recommend to shareholders that you accept Megabook's offer for our company.
9 As you know, Megabook wants to buy this company. As chief financial officer, what do you think of their offer, Saleem?

54.3 A management consultant is talking about meetings, using expressions from C opposite. Put what she says into a logical order.

1 point and rambling. And then there are those who want to show
2 moving. If they do this, it's amazing how much ground you can cover.
3 Of course, everyone wants meetings to be productive and achieve results. But from personal experience, we know that a lot of them are a waste of
4 off: to show how important and clever they are. The chair should keep things
5 the point. And we've all seen those annoying people who keep on wandering off the
6 time, and nothing is achieved. In order for discussion to be useful, people should not go off on digressions: they should stick to

Over to you

What sort of meetings do you go to in your school or organization? Are they useful?

Types of meeting

55 Meetings 2: the role of the chairperson

A Before the meeting

Hilary Rhodes is a management consultant who specializes in meeting skills:

'A good **chairperson** has to be a **good organizer**. What they do before the meeting is as important as the meeting itself. They should make sure the **agenda** (the list of things to be discussed) is complete by asking those involved what should be on it and then **circulating** (distributing) it to everyone concerned. They should check the **venue**, making sure the room will be free, without interruptions, until the end of the meeting.'

B During the meeting

The chairperson should be a **good timekeeper**. They should start the meeting on time, without waiting for **latecomers**.

They should appoint a **minute-taker** to **take the minutes**, making sure that opinions and **action points** (where participants agree to do something) are noted.

They should make sure each point on the agenda is **allocated** the **time** it deserves and should keep to the **timetable**. When the time allocated to one point is up, the chair should make sure that discussion **moves on to the next point**, even if the issue has not been completely covered or **resolved** (decided).

The chair should make sure that each participant has the chance to **make their point**, and should deal **tactfully** with disagreements, making sure that each side feels their point of view has been noted. They should also try to avoid **digressions**, where people get off the point.

Finally, they should ensure the meeting **finishes on time**, or early.

C Follow-up

After some meetings, it's necessary for the minutes to be circulated, especially if there are **action points** that particular people are responsible for.

At the next meeting, the chair should ask for the minutes to be read out and see if all agree that it is an **accurate record** of what happened, and see if there are any **matters arising** (any points from the last meeting that need to be discussed). And they should check what progress has been made on the **action points** from the previous meeting.

55.1 Replace the underlined phrases in this article with the correct expressions from A and B opposite.

I don't know how to chair a meeting!

I've been asked to chair a meeting about the Christmas office party, but I'm incredibly nervous as I've never chaired one before. Is there a secret for success?

You may never have chaired a meeting but as you've probably been to lots you'll have seen it done well and badly. Think about the things that please and annoy you and build on them. (1) Make sure everyone has the agenda well in advance, and check that you know enough about the participants and issues to be discussed. Arrange for the (2) room to be cool rather than warm; people will be less likely to go to sleep.

See yourself as a referee whose job it is to ensure fair play through careful watching and listening. You must ensure that the timid have a chance to (3) say what they want; deal (4) in a diplomatic way with the argumentative and to be kind to the (5) person you have asked to take notes. Getting that individual on your side is essential if you want the record to reflect your desired outcomes. It's normal to suggest what should be left out of the minutes and how any difficult bits should be phrased. Make sure you stick to the (6) time you have allowed for each point and keep things moving by not letting people (7) wander off the subject. Get decisions made and recorded, even if it's only to postpone matters until the next meeting. If someone is being difficult, defuse things by offering to continue the discussion personally at a more appropriate time.

If the meeting is likely to be more than a couple of hours long, try to include a break at the mid-point; it acts as a marker and stops people getting restless.

Aim to leave everyone feeling they have had a chance to say what they wanted to say and gain lasting and well-deserved popularity by finishing (8) when you said the meeting would finish. ■

55.2 Look at A, B and C opposite. Match the verbs (1–7) with the nouns (a–g) that they go with.

1 take	a a minute-taker
2 appoint	b the minutes
3 circulate	c time
4 allocate	d the agenda
5 move on	e to the next point
6 avoid	f on time
7 finish	g digressions

Over to you

What do you think are the most important skills for someone chairing a meeting?

56 Meetings 3: points of view

A Opening the meeting

Carla Eagleton, chief executive of Creative Advertising, is opening a meeting.

She could also have said:

> OK, *let's get started.*

> It's about time we got started.
> Let's begin, shall we?
> Shall we make a start?

> Let's make a start.
> Let's get down to business.

Then she says '**As you know, I've called this meeting to** discuss the situation in the design department. The designers have a lot of freedom to work as they wish, but it seems that things are getting out of control ...'

She could also have said:

- As you are aware ...

- I've arranged this meeting to ...
- The purpose of this meeting is to ...
- The main objective is to ...

B Inviting people to speak

Carla then uses some of these expressions.

Inviting someone to start:

- Would you like to **open the discussion**, Greta?
- Perhaps you'd like to **get the ball rolling**, Greta.
- Greta, would you like to **kick off**?

Asking for one person's opinion:

- **What about you, Keith?**
- **What are your feelings on this, Keith?**
- **What do you think about this, Keith?**
- **What are your views on this, Keith?**

Asking for everyone's opinion:

- What's **the general feeling** on this?

C Making your point

The other participants use some of these expressions.

a Head of human resources: **I believe** the design department needs a certain amount of freedom, but there are limits.

b Head of design: **As I see it**, I can't run the design department as if it was the accounts department.

c Chief financial officer: **In my opinion**, they're going much too far. I can't bear to think of the costs involved.

d Senior designer: **Of course**, we are sensitive types and need to be given the freedom to work how we like.

Making your point

Other ways of making your point include:

- The way I see it ...
- It's clear to me that ...
- Personally, I think ...
- It looks to me as if ...
- Obviously ...

Note: You use **Of course** and **Obviously** to introduce an idea, but also to show that you think other people will be aware of it already. Be careful, as this can sound rude.

56.1 Which of these expressions from A opposite are correct? Correct the mistakes.

1 It's about time we get started.
2 Let's begin, let we?
3 Shall we make a start?
4 Let's do a start.
5 Let's get up to business.
6 I've call this meeting to …
7 The purpose of this meeting is to …
8 The main subject is to …
9 As you are beware …

56.2 Look at B opposite and make these invitations to speak less aggressive and more natural.

1 John, kick off.
2 Kay, open the discussion.
3 Len, get the ball rolling.
4 Monica, tell us what you think.
5 Nigel, give us your views.
6 Olive, what do you feel?

56.3 Match the sentence beginnings (1–5) with the correct endings (a–e). The sentences all contain expressions from C opposite.

1 The way	a I think that the prizes we win help us to attract and keep the best designers.
2 Personally,	b as if the design people think of themselves as living on another planet.
3 It looks to me	c I see it, you should be looking at what we produce, not at the time of day we produce it.
4 It's clear to	d opinion, we have to think of the needs of each department.
5 In my	e me that they set a very bad example to the other departments.

Over to you

How freely can people express their feelings in your school or organization? Are people at all levels encouraged to say what they think? Are new employees asked for their opinions?

57 Meetings 4: agreement and disagreement

A Discussion without argument?

Hilary Rhodes is talking about the importance of keeping calm in meetings:

'In a meeting, you **discuss** things. In the **discussion**, some people may **agree** with you. Others may **disagree**. They may have **differences of opinion** with you, but the important thing is to **keep calm** and remain **courteous**. It's OK to disagree, but it's not OK to be **impolite** or **rude** or to **lose your temper**.

An **argument** is when people disagree about something, perhaps becoming **angry**. **Your argument** is also the set of ideas that you use to **prove your point**: to show that what you are saying is true.'

Note: **Agree** and **disagree** are verbs (e.g. I agree with you, She disagrees with him, etc.). You cannot say ~~I am agree with you~~, ~~She is disagree with him~~, etc.

B Agreeing

Strong agreement:

a **You're perfectly right.** The costs involved must be incredible.
b **I couldn't agree more.** We got our latest recruits after we won the industry award for best advertisement.
c **Precisely.** Creativity comes to some of our people in the middle of the night.
d **Exactly.** We have to look at the company as one unit.
e **Absolutely.** It's the output, not the input, that counts.

Mild agreement:

f **You may be right there.** We're already ten per cent over budget.
g **That's true, I suppose.** There must be some limits on when they work.
h **I suppose so.** They seem to arrive and then go straight out again to eat.

C Disagreeing

Mild disagreement:

a **That's not really how I see it.** Everyone should be allowed to work in the way that's best for them.
b **I don't really agree.** The prizes are important, but people would come to work for us anyway.
c **I can't really go along with you there.** I think we need to see people at their desks actually working.
d **I think you're mistaken.** If the designers get to work late, they don't go out for lunch.
e **I'm afraid I can't agree with you there.** All you financial people do is worry about costs.

Strong disagreement:

f **I'm sorry, but that's out of the question.** You can't expect people to go home at ten and come back at nine in the morning.
g **I think you're wrong.** The design department's costs are justified because of our high quality work. The costs of the other departments are not justified.
h **Of course not.** The latest figures I've seen show that the project is within budget.
i **That's absurd.** There must be some sort of control on when people work.
j **That's ridiculous.** Each department has very specific needs.

Note: Be careful with **That's absurd** and **That's ridiculous**. These expressions are very strong and can be offensive.

57.1 Complete the crossword using the correct form of words from A opposite.

Across

3 The opposite of 'agree'. (8)
7 What you have if you do not agree with someone. (10,2,7)
8 See 2 down.
9 Whatever you do, keep .... (4)
11 When people disagree, they have an ....(8)
12 and 6 down If you want to show you are right, you try to .... your .... (5,5)

Down

1 If you are pleasant and unaggressive, you are .... (9)
2 and 8 across If you become angry, you .... your .... (4,6)
4 The opposite of 'polite'. (8)
5 The noun corresponding to 'angry'. (5)
6 See 12 across.
7 If you talk about something, you .... it. (7)
10 Another word for 4 down. (4)

57.2 Match each statement (1–8) to an appropriate reaction (a–h) from B opposite.

1 And another thing: you should be looking at what we produce, not at the time of day we produce it.
2 Apart from that, if you try to control our working time, we'll lose our creativity.
3 Besides that, the prizes help us to attract and keep the best designers.
4 Even so, I agree that some limits should be set, even if my designers are very different from the accounts people.
5 Not only do we have these very high costs, but it also sets a very bad example to the other departments and they start going over budget too.
6 On the one hand, we have to think of the needs of each department. On the other hand, we have to think of the company as a whole.
7 In addition, our biggest current project looks as though it will be over budget too.
8 What's more, they leave for lunch two hours later.

57.3 Now match the statements (1–8) above with the reactions (a–j) in C opposite.

Over to you

What are you like in meetings? Do you often disagree with other people? Or do you prefer to avoid arguments?

58 Meetings 5: discussion techniques

A   Hedging

Hedging is when you avoid disagreeing directly. To **hedge**, you could say:

- **I take your point** about punctuality, but clocking in and out would not be very popular.
- **I understand what you're saying** about the needs of each department, but each department must be treated in an appropriate way.
- **I see/know what you mean**, but we must look at the human factors as well as the numbers.
- **I hear where you're coming from on this**, but we must remember this is an advertising agency, not a car factory.

B   Checking understanding, interrupting, referring back

To interrupt someone politely:

- **Can I come in here?**
- **If I can just stop you for a moment …**
- **Sorry to interrupt you, but …**

To refer back to what was said earlier:

- **As we were saying earlier …**
- **To go back to what X was saying earlier …**
- **To go back to what I was just saying …**

To check that you understand what someone has said:

- **Are you saying that …?**
- **Are you suggesting that …?**
- **Are you implying that …?**
- **If I understand (you) correctly, …**
- **If I follow you …**

C   Agreement, consensus or compromise?

Hilary Rhodes is talking about how to deal with agreements and disagreements:

'It may be possible to **reach agreement** or **to reach an agreement** about something, or at least **come to a consensus**: something that most people can agree with. It may be possible **to compromise** or to **find a compromise**: an agreement where people accept less than they wanted at first. (See Unit 65) Or perhaps the differences are so great that there will just be **disagreement**. Something in particular that you disagree about is **a disagreement**.'

D   Concluding

Carla Eagleton sums up and brings the meeting to a close:

'Right. I'm afraid **we're running out of time** so **we're going to have to stop there**. **To go over what's been said**, there is a disagreement about timekeeping and budgets in the design department. I've listened to **both sides of the argument**. I think I can **sum it up** by saying that it's a problem of creativity versus control. I think you'll just have to **agree to disagree**. **I'll let you know my decision** about the solution to this problem by the end of the month. So **unless anyone has anything else to add**, I think that's it. Thank you all for coming.'

58.1 Use complete expressions from A and B opposite to complete the dialogue, based on the prompts in brackets. The first one has been done for you.

A: We really will have to increase productivity.

B: (hedge: coming) but there are limits to how much we can ask of each individual employee. After all, if you look back at the records for …

I hear where you're coming from on this, but there are limits to how much we can ask of each individual employee. After all, if you look back at the records for …

A: (interrupt: stop) you have to admit things were different then. That was in the 1980s.

B: (hedge: understand) but that's not so long ago. The pressures were the same.

C: (refer back: go back) there are limits as to what we can ask from the creatives. They …

A: (interrupt: interrupt) I hate that word 'creative'. A lot of them haven't created anything except chaos since they arrived in the company.

C: (check: imply) that the creative department has people who shouldn't be there?

58.2 Put the extracts from this newspaper report of a public meeting into the correct order.

1. a compromise or a consensus. There was total disagreement. After four hours of heated discussion, Ms Johns said, 'It's been a very interesting discussion but we're running

2. out of time and we're going to have to stop there. I'll let you know the committee's decision about the solution to this problem by the end of the month.

3. So unless anyone has anything else to add, I think that's it. A very useful meeting. Thank you all for coming.'

4. There were strong differences of opinion at last night's meeting to discuss banning cars from the centre of Newtown. The chair, Ms Yolanda Johns of the town council's transport committee, organized the meeting well. A lot of ground

5. saying it would improve the quality of life. It was not possible to come to

6. was covered and both sides of the argument were heard. To sum up the arguments, there were those who thought that banning cars would damage shops and businesses in the town. Others disagreed,

Over to you

Are compromises always possible? In your organization or school, are decisions based on compromise and consensus or are they imposed by the management?

59 Presentations 1: preparation and introduction

A Types of presentation

Melanie Kray is an expert in giving presentations.
Here, she gives some examples of different presentations:

- **press conference:** two chief executives tell journalists why their companies have merged.
- **briefing:** a senior officer gives information to other officers about a police operation they are about to undertake.
- **demonstration:** the head of research and development tells non-technical colleagues about a new machine.
- **product launch:** a car company announces a new model.
- **lecture:** a university professor communicates information about economics to 300 students.
- **talk:** a member of a stamp-collecting club tells other members about 19th century British stamps.
- **seminar:** a financial adviser gives advice about investments to eight people.
- **workshop:** a yoga expert tells people how to improve their breathing techniques and gets them to practise.

A briefing

B Dos and don'ts: preparation

Here are some tips for a **stand-up presentation** (one person talking to an audience).

a Find out about the **audience:** how many people there will be, who they are, why they will be there, and how much they know about the subject.
b Find out about the **venue** and the **facilities:** the room, the seating plan, the equipment, etc.
c Plan the **content** and **structure**, but don't write the complete text of the presentation.
d Write notes on sheets of paper, not on **cards.**
e Try to **memorize** the first five sentences of your talk.
f Prepare **visual aids:** pictures, diagrams, etc.
g **Rehearse** your presentation (practise it so that it becomes very familiar) with friends or colleagues.

C Key phrases: introduction

Melanie is advising Anne-Marie Duval on giving a presentation at a conference.

h **Introduce** yourself and your subject.

> My name's Anne-Marie Duval and I work for Gem Consultants. My talk is called 'Consultancy Skills for the 21st Century'.

i **Outline** what you're going to talk about: describe the different sections of your talk.

> There are three main skills areas I want to talk about today …

j Say whether people should ask **questions** during the talk, or at the end.

> If you have any questions, I'll be very happy to answer them at the end of the session.

A seminar

A product launch

A workshop

A lecture

59.1 Match the presentation types in A opposite to the things (1–8) that people say in them.

1 As you can see, this prototype is far in advance of anything we've done before.
2 Here are some typical patterns for demand and supply in the widget industry.
3 I'm going to give each group a series of problems faced by an imaginary company, and I want you to suggest solutions.
4 Now is the right time to get out of company shares and invest in property.
5 The combined resources of our two organizations will allow us to achieve great things.
6 The first postage stamp in the world was the Penny Black in 1840.
7 The parachutists will come in at 08:30 and land in two waves, here and here.
8 The X300 has the most advanced features of any car in its class.

59.2 Here are reasons for the advice given in B and C opposite. Match each reason (1–10) to a piece of advice (a–j).

1 If you drop the cards on the floor, you're in trouble.
2 It could sound monotonous and boring if you speak from a complete, prepared text.
3 It will help you adjust the content of your talk so that it is suitable, for example not too easy or difficult.
4 It will help you to keep control, and avoid people interrupting if you don't want them to.
5 It will help your audience follow the logic of what you're going to say.
6 It will make you feel more at ease at the beginning, when you may be nervous.
7 It will reassure people that they are in the right place, and provide a focus for the beginning of your talk.
8 They add visual interest, provide you with support and help the audience follow you.
9 You can ask for changes in the seating plan if necessary.
10 They will be able to tell you if anything is unclear before the presentation.

Over to you

Have you ever given a presentation? What type was it?
In your experience, what makes a good/bad presentation?

60 Presentations 2: main part

A Dos and don'ts: timing

Melanie Kray is giving more advice about presentations.

a Start on time. Don't wait for **latecomers**.

b Plan how long you're going to spend on each point and keep to these **timings**.

c Don't **labour** a particular point (spend too long on something).

d Don't **digress** (talk about things that have nothing to do with the subject), unless you have a particular purpose in mind.

e Finish on time. Don't **run over**. It looks bad if you don't have time to finish all your points and answer questions.

B Dos and don'ts: voice

f **Project** your voice to the back of the room, but don't shout. Don't ask if people at the back can hear. Check the volume (loudness) of your voice beforehand.

g Use a **microphone** if you need one. Don't hold it too close to your mouth.

h Whether using a microphone or not, speak in a **natural tone of voice**. Don't speak in a **monotone** (on the same level all the time). Vary the **pitch** (level) of your voice.

C Rapport with the audience

Experts say that you can **gain the audience's attention** in a presentation by:

- telling an **anecdote** (a story, perhaps a personal one).

- mentioning a *really* surprising **fact** or **statistic**.

- stating a **problem**.

- asking a **question**.

Of course, it is important to respect the cultural expectations of your audience. (See Units 45–7)

D Key phrases: main part

Anne-Marie continues her presentation:

'OK. **To begin, let's look at** the first type of skills that consultants need: technical skills. **Of course**, related to technical skills is a good general knowledge of management subjects ... But **I'm digressing: let's get back** to the technical skills themselves ... **That's all I have time for on** technical skills.

Let's move on to the second area: interpersonal skills. **As you can see** on this transparency, there are two **key areas in relation to** interpersonal skills ... I think **that covers everything on** interpersonal skills.

Time is moving on, so let's turn to the third area: people management issues.'

60.1 Melanie recently went to a presentation where the speaker did not follow her advice. Match each of Melanie's thoughts (1–7) to the points (a–h) in A and B opposite.

1 Why is he yelling like that? The room's not that big!

2 He's already said that three times.

3 I know there are people who want to ask questions, and there won't be time.

4 He's really droning on: there's no life in his voice and everyone's asleep.

5 The sound of his breath in the microphone is really annoying.

6 I don't see what this has got to do with what he's trying to say.

7 Get on with it! If people turn up late, that's their problem.

60.2 Look at D opposite and correct the mistakes in these sentences.

1 OK. For begin , let we look for the most basic product in our range.

2 Of course, related with product specifications of our basic model is the issue of product performance.

3 But I'm a digression : let's get back on the product specifications themselves.

4 That's all I'm having time for on product specifications. Let's moving on to our mid-range model.

5 As you can be seeing on this transparency, there are two key features I want to talk about in relative to our mid-range model.

6 I think that covers up everything on our mid-range model.

7 Time is moved on , so let's turn up to our top-of-the-range product.

Over to you

How are people expected to dress for different types of presentation in your country? What do people think about humour in presentations?

61 Presentations 3: closing and questions

A Dos and don'ts: body language

Melanie gives these tips on body language.

- Make **eye contact**: look at each person in the audience for about a second, before moving on to the next person. Don't concentrate on just one or two people.
- Don't speak to the equipment or the screen: **face the audience** at all times.
- **Smiling** is fine at appropriate moments, but not too much.
- Use **gesture** (hand movements) to emphasize key points.
- Stay more or less in one place: don't move around too much.
- Avoid **mannerisms** (ways of moving and speaking which you do repeatedly without realizing).

B Visual aids

Melanie sometimes uses these visual aids when giving presentations:

C Key phrases: closing and dealing with questions

Anne-Marie is bringing her presentation to a close:

'Let me **sum up**. **Firstly**, we looked at technical skills, **secondly**, at management skills and **last, but by no means least**, at interpersonal skills. **In my view**, the secret for success in the future is going to be interpersonal skills. **That brings me to the end** of my presentation. **Are there any questions**?'

Here are some phrases which can be useful when answering questions:

a **That's a fair point.** I know that some consultants don't have a very good image. But I think that Gem Consultants have helped companies reduce costs and increase profits enormously.
b **That's confidential.** I'm afraid I'm not at liberty to tell you.
c **That's not really my field.** But I can put you in touch with someone in my organization who is working on Internet applications.
d **The questioner would like to know** what sort of background the people we recruit usually have. Is that right?
e **Well, I think that goes beyond the scope of today's presentation.** Today I wanted to concentrate on consultants' skills, not go into particular case studies in consultancy.
f **I'm afraid we've run out of time.** But if you'd like to come and discuss that with me now, I'll try and give you an answer.

If a member of the audience didn't hear a question, they might say:

'**Sorry, I didn't catch the question** – could you repeat what the questioner said?'

Anne-Marie ends the presentation by saying:

'I think that's a good place to stop. Thank you for listening.'

61.1 Which words from A and B opposite could the underlined words refer to? In some cases there is more than one possible answer.

1 But don't overdo <u>it</u>. It can seem insincere (not real).
2 Again, don't overdo <u>it</u>. Look round at everybody in the room.
3 Don't let <u>these</u> dominate the presentation. People have come to see you, not the equipment.
4 Do not use continuous text on <u>these</u>.
5 Do not use <u>one</u> in a large room because people at the back won't be able to see it.
6 Don't look at <u>it</u> or the screen behind you: face the audience at all times.
7 Have a backup plan if <u>it</u> fails to work.
8 Keep <u>them</u> under control. Remember, for example, that pointing with your finger is rude in some cultures.
9 Make sure there will be enough of <u>them</u> for everyone and make sure that they reach everyone in the room as some people tend to keep them without handing them on.
10 Some of <u>them</u>, for example putting your hands in your pockets or running your fingers through your hair, really upset some people.

61.2 Match these questions from the audience (1–6) to the answers (a–f) that Anne-Marie gives in C opposite.

1 Sorry, I didn't catch the end of the question – could you repeat what the questioner said?
2 In what ways do you think the Internet is going to change the way management consultants work in the future?
3 Some companies refuse to use management consultants. What do you say to people who say that consultants are a waste of time and money?
4 What's the average salary for your consultants?
5 I don't know if you have time to answer this, but can you tell me how I can apply to work for Gem?
6 You say that Gem have enormously increased profits for some companies. Can you give one or two examples of this?

Over to you

How is body language used in presentations in your country? Which gestures are acceptable and which are not?

What are the advantages and disadvantages of using different types of equipment? What are some of the potential problems?

62 Negotiations 1: situations and negotiators

A Types of negotiation

If people **negotiate** (**with each other**), they talk in order to reach an agreement which is to their **mutual advantage** (good for them both). For example:

- **customer–supplier negotiations**
- **wage negotiations**
- **merger** or **takeover negotiations**
- **trade negotiations**

Negotiations also take place to **settle disputes** (decide arguments) such as:

- **contract disputes**
- **labour disputes**
- **trade disputes**

B Word combinations with 'negotiations'

Intense / Intensive		are very difficult and tiring, with a lot being discussed.
Delicate / Tense	negotiations	are very difficult and could easily fail.
Eleventh-hour / Last-minute		take place at the last possible moment of the time available.
Protracted		take a very long time.

Someone who takes part in negotiations is a **negotiator**, and someone who is good at getting what they want is a **tough negotiator**.

C Bargaining

Another word for 'negotiate' is **bargain**. This is also used to talk specifically about discussing and agreeing the price of something. Another name for 'negotiator' is **bargainer**.

Another word for 'negotiation' is **bargaining**, used especially in phrases like:

- **collective bargaining**
- **pay bargaining**
- **wage bargaining** (discussions between groups of employees and their employers about pay and conditions)

'Bargaining' is often used in these combinations:

bargaining	ploy / tactic	a particular technique used by a negotiator
	chip / tool	an issue that a negotiator uses in order to gain an advantage
	point	a particular issue that a negotiator discusses
	power	the degree to which one side is strong enough to obtain what it wants
	process	the way that negotiations develop

62.1 Relate these headlines to the situations in A opposite.

1
CAR WORKERS IN TWO-YEAR PAY DEAL TALKS WITH FORD

2
FRANCE BANS US FILMS FOLLOWING TALKS BREAKDOWN

3
WORLD TRADE ORGANIZATION MEMBERS IN WIDE-RANGING DISCUSSIONS

4
EMPLOYERS REFUSE TO NEGOTIATE WITH STRIKING MINERS

5
EUROTUNNEL ATTACKS CONSTRUCTION COMPANIES FOR LATE COMPLETION

6
PHARMACEUTICAL GIANTS SAY THAT COMBINING WOULD BE 'TO THEIR MUTUAL ADVANTAGE'

7
EDUCATION MINISTRY AND COMPAQ IN 'COMPUTER ON EVERY DESK' TALKS

62.2 Match the sentence beginnings (1–8) with the correct endings (a–h). The sentences all contain expressions from B and C opposite.

1 After 48 hours of intensive negotiations in which he slept for

2 One of the problems of protracted negotiations is that achieving agreement can come

3 After tense negotiations between the hijackers and air traffic control in Cyprus,

4 The agreement on limiting television violence represents the climax of several months of intense

5 The painting has been withdrawn from sale and acquired by the National Gallery

6 Then violence broke out, and it took six months

7 The deal was struck only after eleventh-

8 He's a tough negotiator

a the plane was allowed to land at Larnaca airport.

b hour negotiations between the US, the European Union and Japan.

c only one hour, Mr Prescott said, 'It has been both tough and incredibly complicated.'

d of delicate negotiations to put the process back on track.

e negotiations between television executives and the National Parent Teacher Association.

f to be more important than anything else, including the final decision.

g and likes bargaining about everything.

h after last-minute negotiations with the auctioneers, Sotheby's.

Over to you

What qualities make a good negotiator?

Do you have to negotiate? Do you like negotiating? Why / why not?

63 Negotiations 2: preparing

A Preparing to negotiate

John Rix is an expert on negotiation:

'Before negotiations begin, preparing and planning are very important.

a Get as much information as possible about the situation. If dealing with people from another culture, find out about its **etiquette** and **negotiating styles**: the way people negotiate, what they consider to be acceptable and unacceptable behaviour, and so on. (See Unit 45)

b Work out your initial **bargaining position**: what are your **needs** and **objectives** (the things that you want to achieve)? Decide your **priorities** (the most important objectives).

c Try to estimate the needs and objectives of the other side.

d Prepare a **fallback position**: conditions that you will accept if your original objectives are not met.

e Perhaps you are in a position to influence the choice of **venue**: the place where you are going to meet. If so, would you prefer to:
- **be on your own ground / on home ground** (in your own offices)
- go to see the other side **on their ground** (in their offices)
- meet on **neutral ground**, for example in a hotel?

f If you are negotiating as part of a **negotiating team,** consult your colleagues about points a to e, and allocate roles and responsibilities.'

B Negotiating scenario

At the beginning of a negotiation, follow these steps:

 Meet and greet **representatives** of the other company and introduce your colleagues.

 Offer coffee and **small talk**. Try to create a **relaxed atmosphere.**

 Go to the meeting room and suggest that you **get down to business.**

 Have a clear **agenda** and a **timetable.** (See Unit 55)

 First, give the **background** to the negotiations. Talking about the situation is a good way of reminding people of key facts and issues.

 Then **kick off** the negotiations themselves, perhaps by finding out more about the priorities of the other side (the things they think are most important) or talking about your own requirements.

C Negotiating styles

When you're negotiating with people from other cultures, it's important to think about what they consider as 'normal' behaviour. (See Units 45–7) You'll need to think about the following:

- body language
- physical contact
- conversational rules
- relationship building
- hierarchy
- attitudes to time

63.1 José Oliveira is head of Xania, a Brazilian aircraft manufacturer. He is preparing for negotiations with Zebra, an engine supplier. Match each point (1–6) in José's notes with one of the tips (a–f) in A opposite.

1 organize preparatory meeting with head of manufacturing and head of purchasing to discuss strategy
2 persuade Zebra representatives to come to our offices in São Paulo
3 principal objective: delivery of first 20 engines in six months; other objectives: flexible payment, strong quality guarantees; price less important, but aim for US$500,000 per engine; find out more about Zebra's priorities
4 rumour says that Zebra are in financial difficulty: they badly need orders
5 will accept price up to US$550,000 if specifications are good
6 Zebra well-known in the industry for its 'strong' negotiating techniques

63.2 Look at the steps in B opposite. Arrange these phrases José uses at the beginning of the negotiation in the correct order.

1 As you all probably know, Mr Watanabe and I met at the Aerospace Trade Fair in Frankfurt last year and we had a very interesting discussion about the possibility of our two companies working together.
2 I believe you're flying back on Friday evening, so that gives us three days. I think two days should be enough to cover all the points. On the third day, Friday, if we have an agreement, I'll ask our lawyers to finalize conditions for the contract with you.
3 Mr Watanabe, good to see you again. How are you? Let me introduce my colleagues: Sandra Lisboa, our chief purchasing officer, and this is Fernando dos Santos, head of production at Xania.
4 Shall we go to the conference room and make a start?
5 Well we've looked at the potential market for our new plane, and it looks as if we will need 100 engines over the next three years.
6 Would you like some coffee or tea, or would you prefer juice? How was the flight?

63.3 Mr A is in another country in order to try and get a multi-million dollar order from Mr B and his assistant, Mr C. Put each problem that occurs in their meeting under one or more of the headings in C opposite.

1 Mr A wanted to start the negotiations immediately, but Mr B suggested a sightseeing tour of the city and a game of golf the next day.
2 Mr B started asking Mr A about his wife, home and family.
3 When Mr C made an important point, Mr A was silent for two minutes before replying. This made Mr C very nervous.
4 When talking, Mr B looked directly at Mr A and his two assistants in turn, giving them equal attention. Mr A started to look annoyed.
5 During a break for coffee, Mr B put his arm around Mr A's shoulders in order to be friendly.
6 When Mr A was talking, Mr C frequently interrupted him.

Over to you

What are the normal social 'rules' in your country in the context of a buyer-customer negotiation?

64 Negotiations 3: furthering negotiations

A Win–win

In a successful negotiation, everyone should leave the negotiating table happy with the outcome: there shouldn't be winners and losers. The negotiators should try to reach a **win–win solution**: an agreement of equal benefit to both sides. This can be achieved in a number of ways.

B Probing

One way of furthering negotiations is **probing** (asking the right questions and listening carefully to the answers). Here are some probing questions:

a What is the situation on production at your plant at the moment?
b What sort of quantities are you looking for?
c What are we looking at in the way of discount?
d What did you have in mind regarding specifications?
e What were you thinking of in terms of delivery dates?
f How important to you is the currency for payment?

C Proposal and counter-proposal

Through a series of proposals or offers from one side and **counter-proposals** or **counter-offers** from the other side, the two sides work towards an agreement which will benefit them both.

Here are some ways of making offers:

If you offer more flexible payment conditions,		**be able to** (+ infinitive)
As long as engine performance improves by ten per cent,	will	**agree to** (+ infinitive)
On condition that you deliver 20 engines by May,	can	
Supposing that you provide good technical support,	could	**consider** (+ -ing)
Provided that you supply documentation in Portuguese,	may	**offer** (+ noun)
Providing that this contract works out OK,	might	**offer to** (+ infinitive)

then we ...

D Trade-offs

When you offer to change your position to one that is less favourable to yourself, you **make a concession**. Perhaps this is in exchange for a **concession** from the other side, although there is no guarantee of this. Your concession may be a **goodwill gesture**: a concession that you make hoping that the other side will see this as friendly and make a concession in return.

Even in a friendly negotiation, there may be **horse-trading**, with each side making a series of concessions in return for concessions from the other side. (This expression is often used to show disapproval.) If you argue about something for a long time, especially about the price of something, you **haggle**.

A series of concessions in exchange for concessions from the other side is a series of **trade-offs**. If you make a concession, you may not get anything back. If you make a **trade-off**, you give something away and get something in return.

64.1 Match the replies (1–6) to the probing questions (a–f) in B opposite.

1 Perhaps 100 units per year over five years.
2 We can offer ten per cent if the quantities are right.
3 We'd like to see a ten per cent improvement in performance.
4 We'd prefer US dollars.
5 We'll need the first 30 units in six months.
6 We're operating at full capacity.

64.2 The Xania–Zebra negotiations continue. Use expressions from C opposite to complete José's phrases below, using the correct form of the words in brackets. The first one has been done for you.

1 If you offer more flexible payment conditions, might / consider pay / higher price.
If you offer more flexible payment conditions, then we might consider paying a higher price.
2 As long as engine performance improves by ten per cent, may / offer / price / $550,000 per unit.
3 On condition that you deliver 20 engines by May, will / be able to / consider / more flexible / price.
4 Supposing that you provide good technical support, might / be able to / increase / order.
5 Provided that you supply documentation in Portuguese, could / consider / send personnel / you / training.
6 Providing that this contract works out OK, might / agree / work / you / future.

64.3 Use expressions from D opposite to complete these extracts.

1 The Government's approach of 'If you do this, then we'll do that' seems to owe more to political .... than good policy-making.

2 When London was chosen as the site of the European Bank for Reconstruction and Development, France insisted that a Frenchman get the top job. When Frankfurt was chosen for the European Central Bank, the French again wanted a similar ....

3 The unions suspended the strike until next week as a goodwill .... aimed at reopening negotiations with employers' organizations on ending the strike.

4 She is a hard, unforgiving businesswoman making .... to no one.

5 When too many customers turn up, some airlines have introduced compensation packages to persuade them to take a later flight. Experienced travellers then .... to get an even better package.

Over to you

Is every negotiation potentially a win–win one?

Do you think that making goodwill gestures is a good idea, or should you always demand concessions in return for the concessions that you make?

65 Negotiations 4: difficulties

A Confrontation

Sometimes one side is in a stronger position than the other: they have more **bargaining power**. For example, during a recent strike at Lamda Inc., the company was in financial difficulty and the public was on the workers' side, so Lamda was **negotiating from weakness**. The strikers' union knew this: they were **negotiating from strength**.

The union made **demands**: objectives that were so important that they were unwilling to change them. They wanted a 15 per cent pay increase. Later they **moderated** these demands, and said they would accept ten per cent. However, their demand for a week's extra holiday was **non-negotiable**: they would not accept less.

Lamda said they were being forced to accept something that they did not want. They accused the union of making them negotiate **under duress**.

Eventually Lamda **conceded** to most of the union's demands and gave them what they wanted. The media said that Lamda had **backed down**, **climbed down** and **given in**.

The feelings had been very strong on each side: the **dispute** was **bitter**, and the negotiations were **confrontational** and **adversarial**.

A strike

B Confrontational negotiating tactics

Although using **tricks** isn't recommended, there are negotiators who:

- issue **threats**, **final offers** or **ultimatums**: they say that the other side must accept something, with very bad consequences for them if they refuse.
- lie and **bluff**: they threaten to do something that they do not intend to do, or are not able to do.

Of course, you can always **call someone's bluff**: pretend to believe them, when you know they are bluffing.

C Dealing with problems

When negotiations get stuck, and don't progress, there are a number of things you can do.

a Underline **common ground**: the areas where agreement has been reached.
b **Reassure** the other side on key points that have been decided: confirm that you have not changed your mind.
c Be willing to **compromise** on your original objectives: be ready to accept less than you wanted in exchange for compromises from the other side.
d Identify the exact **obstacles** or **sticking points**: the problems that are causing negotiations to become difficult.
e **Postpone** discussions until later so that each side can **reconsider its position**.

65.1 Look at A opposite. Which expression best describes each of these statements about a miner's strike? Sometimes there is more than one possible answer.

1 Of course, the company had enormous stocks of coal that had already been produced but not sold and it suited them if there was no more production for six months.
2 The union wasn't in a good position. Apart from the enormous coal stocks, there are thousands of people already out of work.
3 In the beginning, the union said they wanted a pay increase of 100 per cent, and nothing less was acceptable, but later they realized this was unrealistic, and said they would accept less.
4 Eventually the miners went back to work. The strike had produced nothing for them.
5 Of course, the mining company had been very aggressive towards the miners.

65.2 Match the sentence beginnings (1–5) with the correct endings (a–e). The sentences all contain expressions from B opposite.

1 Boeing offered the idea of a 600-plus seat jet to airlines last autumn.	a for example, allowing only whole chickens to be imported, not chicken parts.
2 The country's trade negotiators are trying all sorts of tricks to protect their farmers,	b But European plane industry executives are convinced that Boeing is bluffing.
3 The TV presenter gave his bosses an ultimatum that he would leave the show	c the last one being £28,000 to each docker involved in the dispute.
4 The company said they would fire all of us if we didn't accept the deal	d if Miss Taylor was allowed to stay as co-presenter.
5 Over the past two years, Mersey Docks has made a number of 'final' offers,	e but we called their bluff – we refused and six months later we still have our jobs!

65.3 José Oliveira is trying to deal with some problems in the Xania–Zebra negotiations. Match the expressions (1–5) to the points (a–e) in C opposite.

1 With currency values changing so quickly, you want to think further about the currency you want to be paid in.
2 If you can increase the performance of the type of engine we're interested in, we may be willing to pay a little more.
3 Well, the currency for payment would seem to be the problem here.
4 We've reached agreement on the number of engines you are willing to buy, and that's very positive.
5 We've definitely reached a consensus on price – that much at least is agreed.

Over to you

Do you think people should tell the complete truth when negotiating?

66 Negotiations 5: reaching agreement

A Deadlock and mediators

BASEBALL STRIKE IN BASELAND

Every year in Baseland there are negotiations between the baseball players' union and the baseball team owners about pay and conditions for the coming season. Last year, after months of negotiations, there was **deadlock**: the negotiations **broke down**. Some commentators said there was **stalemate**; an **impasse**: a situation where no progress could be made. There were **irreconcilable differences** between the two sides and it was impossible to reach an agreement. The baseball players went on strike.

The two sides agreed to bring in a **mediator**, someone from outside to help restart the negotiations and bring the two sides closer together in a process of **mediation**. The person they chose was a respected retired politician. He recommended a **cooling-off period** where each side would take no action. The players ended their strike for the time being.

Another month passed, and still there was no progress. The two sides agreed to accept an agreement imposed by an **arbitrator**. A judge was chosen. She looked at the claims of each side and imposed a **settlement** or **resolution** to the dispute, fixing the salaries and the working conditions of the players. In this case, **arbitration** had settled the dispute.

B Agreements and contracts

An agreement of any kind is a **deal**. When you reach an agreement, you can talk about **clinching a deal** or **closing a deal**.

A **bargain** is also an agreement reached through negotiation. People who get what they want in a negotiation are said to **drive a hard bargain**.

An agreement may be in the form of a **contract**.

'Contract' is used in these combinations:

A/An	**employment** **labour** (BrE) **labor** (AmE)	contract	is about what someone has to do in their job, or about what a particular group of employees have to do.
	oral / verbal		is not written down.
	binding **legal**		forces both sides to carry out the actions that they had promised to carry out, by law.
	commercial		is about buying or selling a product

C Checking the deal

It's important to check the points of an agreement to avoid misunderstandings. You could say:

- **Let me just go/run over** (repeat and summarize) the main points.
- **On A,** we agreed that …
- **As far as B is concerned** (in relation to B), we agreed …
- **We still have the question of C to settle** (decide and agree on).
- And there's still the **outstanding** (remaining undecided) **issue** of D.
- We'll send you a **written proposal**.
- We'll **draw up** (write) a **contract** based on those points.
- **I think that covers everything.**

66.1 Look at the words from A opposite and say if these statements are true or false.

1 Someone who helps two sides to reach an agreement is an arbitrator.
2 If two sides in a dispute use arbitration, no outsiders are involved.
3 It's not usual for mediators to impose agreements.
4 If you're in an impasse, you think that progress is possible.
5 If negotiations break down, they stop.
6 Irreconcilable differences are not important.
7 If the two sides agree on a cooling-off period of one week, negotiations continue the next day.

66.2 Complete these extracts using word combinations from B opposite.

1 Buyer and seller enter into a legally .... contract once an offer has been accepted.

2 DAF is bidding for a .... contract to supply trucks to the British army.

3 If two people have agreed on something and signed a sheet of paper, is that a .... contract?

4 Peters claimed that Schaffer was only an employee in his company, but Schaffer asserted that an unwritten, ... contract made them partners.

5 She had an .... contract due to expire later in the year and wanted to take time off work to have children.

66.3 The Xania–Zebra negotiations are ending. Look at C opposite. Arrange the phrases José uses to close negotiations in the correct order.

1 Let me just run over the main points. On engine quantities,
2 I think that covers everything.
3 If you agree to the proposal, we'll draw up a contract based on those points.
4 payment to settle, and there is also still the outstanding issue of documentation.
5 we agreed that you would improve the power of the engine by ten per cent.
6 we agreed that you would supply us with 120 units over four years. As far as performance is concerned,
7 We still have the question of the currency for
8 We'll send you a written proposal on these last two issues.

Over to you

What sort of agreements or contracts does your organization or school have with others? Who draws them up?

Think of some recent negotiations in your country. What stages did they go through?

Answer key

1.1 I work for a French supermarket company. I work on the development of new supermarkets. In fact, I run the development department and I manage a team looking at the possibilities in different countries. It's very interesting. One of my main responsibilities is to make sure that new supermarkets open on time. I'm also in charge of financial reporting.

I deal with a lot of different organizations in my work. I'm responsible for planning projects from start to finish. I work closely with our foreign partners, so I travel a lot.

1.2
1 to
2 to
3 at
4 off
5 in
6 out of

1.3
2 He has a full-time job.
3 She works full-time.
4 I work part-time.
5 She has a permanent job.
6 He has a temporary job.
7 She has temporary work.

2.1 1b, 2e, 3d, 4a, 5c

2.2
1b working, boring, involves
2c being/to be
3a travelling, tiring, dealing
4d tiring
5e stimulating, repetitive

3.1

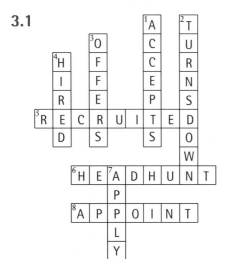

3.2
1 recruit, headhunt, appoint, offer, hire
2 accept, turn down, apply

3.3
1 turned down
2 an interview
3 his referees
4 offered him the job
5 accepted
6 applications
7 CVs
8 applicants
9 their qualifications
10 had shortlisted six people and given them psychometric tests

4.1
1 At 18, Ravi decided to stay in full-time education and went to Mumbai University.
2 Ravi graduated three years later with a degree in philosophy and politics.
3 He taught for a while, but didn't like it. He decided to train as an accountant at evening classes.
4 He qualified as an accountant and joined a big accountancy firm in its Mumbai office.
5 When he started, he needed to develop other skills, which would come through experience.
6 He received management training to help him develop these skills.

4.2
1 skilled	5 unskilled
2 highly skilled	6 unskilled
3 semi-skilled	7 semi-skilled
4 highly skilled	8 skilled

4.3
1 numerate
2 motivated, driven
3 organized, methodical, systematic
4 talented, motivated
5 computer-literate, proactive, self-starter, team-player

5.1
2 overtime, commission	5 company car
3 bonus	6 pension
4 company perks	7 benefits package

5.2
1 severance payment, severance package
2 compensation package, remuneration package
3 performance-related bonus
4 fat cats

6.1

Crossword:
2 across: WHITE
5 across: STAFF
7 across: MANUAL
8 across: STRIKE
10 across: EMPLOYEE
11 across: OUT
13 across: PERSONNEL
14 across: LABOUR
17 across: COLLAR
18 across: INDUSTRIAL

1 down: PAYROLL
3 down: UNION
4 down: BLUE
5 down: SHRLF (SHARE...)
6 down (2 down): WORKFORCE
9 down: STOP
12 down: SLOW
15 down: ACTION
16 down: G

6.2
1 office
2 head office
3 headquarters
4 open-plan
5 administrative staff
6 support
7 human resources department
8 HRD

7.1

Noun – Verb	Noun – Adjective
retirement – retire	seniority – senior
demotion – demote	freelance, freelancer – freelance
lay-off – lay off	redundancy – redundant
dismissal – dismiss	insecurity – insecure
termination – terminate	flexibility – flexible

7.2 1b, 2d, 3e, 4c, 5a

7.3
1 reviews
2 off
3 contracts
4 freelancers
5 laying
6 flatter
7 leaner
8 redundant
9 outplacement

8.1 1b, 2c, 3a, 4f, 5e, 6d

8.2
1 bullying
2 sexual harassment, harassed
3 glass ceiling, sex discrimination
4 racial discrimination, racist, discriminated
5 affirmative action, affirmative action

9.1
1 marketing director
2 research director
3 marketing director
4 human resources director
5 customer services manager
6 sales manager

9.2

Montebello	Gomi	Jones
President and CEO	Non-executive director	Non-executive director

Smith	Chang	Roberts	Dawes
CFO	VP Marketing	VP Research	VP Human Resources

10.1
1 entrepreneurs
2 entrepreneurial
3 founded
4 start-up
5 grow
6 leadership
7 empire

10.2
Hearst: press magnate
Son: software tycoon
Trump: property tycoon
Murdoch: media mogul
Onassis: shipping magnate
Getty: oil mogul

11.1
1 Before we employ people, we like to put them in job situations to see how they do the work and fit into the corporate culture.
2 The company has built a grand corporate headquarters as a permanent symbol of its power.
3 Our stylish new corporate logo shows our wish to be seen as a more international airline.
4 The economy is growing and corporate profits are rising.
5 The rules were introduced to protect women working in factories, but today they make it harder for women to climb the corporate ladder.
6 Companies hit by computer crime are not talking about it because they fear the publicity will harm their corporate image.

11.2
1 commercial airline
2 commercial land
3 commercial television
4 commercial artist
5 commercial disaster

11.3
1 free enterprise
2 private enterprise
3 enterprise economy
3 corporation
4 enterprise culture
5 enterprise zone

12.1
1 partnership
2 public limited company
3 corporation
4 sole owner, freelancer
5 limited company

12.2
1 demutualization
2 Building Society
3 members
4 demutualized
5 demutualize
6 mutual

12.3   1b, 2c, 3e, 4a, 5d

13.1
1 property
2 telecommunications
3 cars
4 tourism
5 financial services
6 defence
7 leisure
8 pharmaceuticals
9 media
10 healthcare

13.2

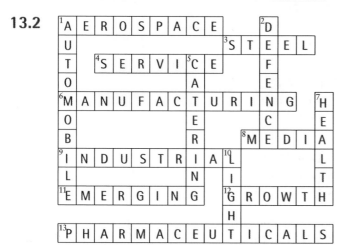

14.1
1 (a) Market research showed, (b) beta version, (c) after the launch
2 (d) the focus groups, (e) safe, (f) industrial scale
3 (g) designers, (h) testing, (i) CADCAM

14.2
1 design
2 market
3 groups
4 consumer
5 surveys
6 product launch
7 design
8 recall

15.1
1 a design
2 design
3 development
4 a development
5 an invention
6 an invention
7 innovation
8 an innovation

15.2
1 and
2 of
3 development
4 the
5 and
6 at
7 research
8 laboratories
9 some
10 innovative
11 in
12 made
13 breakthroughs
14 technology
15 to
16 The
17 of
18 is
19 of
20 leading
21 is
22 knowledge

15.3 1c, 2f, 3d, 4e, 5a, 6b

16.1 manufacture, manufacturer, manufacturing, manufactured goods
produce: non-food, producer, production, product
produce: food, producer, production, produce

16.2 3, 2, 4, 7, 1, 5, 6, 8

16.3 1b, 2f, 3g, 4e, 5d, 6c, 7a

17.1

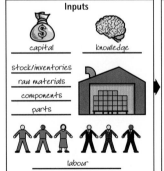 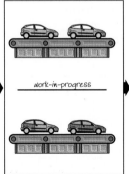 

17.2 1c, 2a, 3d, 4b

17.3
1 just-in-time
2 warehouses
3 to finance
4 store
5 more efficient
6 lean manufacturing

18.1

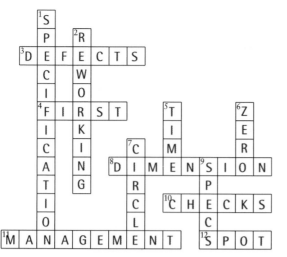

18.2
1 continuous improvement
2 business process re-engineering
3 benchmarking
4 best practice
5 continuous improvement

19.1
1 buyer, consumer, customer
2 customer base
3 client
4 client base, clientele
5 seller
6 seller, vendor
7 buyer, purchaser
8 vendor
9 buyer, purchaser, buying manager, purchasing manager
10 user, end-user

19.2

1 place	3 prices	5 forces
2 reforms	4 pressures	6 economy

20.1

1 penetrate	3 corner, driving out
2 entered, dominated	4 monopolized

20.2
1 are the market leader
2 have a 55 per cent market share
3 Market growth is
4 market segments
5 market segmentation

20.3

1 500	3 A	5 B, C, D and E
2 yes	4 A and B	6 no

21.1
1 product, price, place, promotion
2 no
3 no

21.2 1d, 2e, 3a, 4c, 5b

22.1 1g, 2f, 3e, 4c, 5d, 6b, 7a

22.2
1 consumer durables
2 raw materials
3 consumer durables
4 fast-moving consumer goods
5 fast-moving consumer goods

22.3
1 brand manager
2 brand
3 brand recognition
4 brand image
5 own-brand
6 generic products
7 branded

23.1
1 true
2 true
3 true
4 false
5 true
6 false
7 true

23.2
1 hike
2 boom
3 cuts
4 controls
5 leader
6 tag
7 war

23.3
1 entry-level
2 trade up
3 move upmarket
4 sophisticated
5 mid-ranged
6 top-en
7 niche market

24.1
1 distribution channel
2 wholesalers
3 retailers
4 resellers
5 customer
6 middleman

24.2
1 shopping mall
2 shopping centre
3 convenience store
4 drugstore
5 deep discounter
6 department store

24.3
1 junk mail
2 call centre
3 mailshot
4 cold call
5 direct marketing
6 telemarketing

25.1

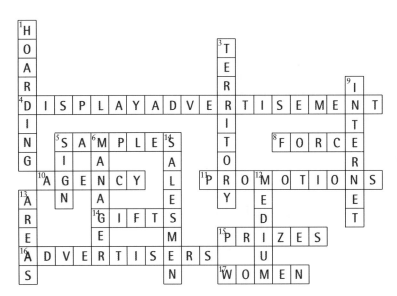

25.2 1b, 2a, 3c

26.1 1c, 2a, 3b, 4f, 5d, 6e

26.2
1 bricks-and-mortar / traditional retailing
2 clicks-and-mortar / e-commerce
3 shopping cart
4 last mile problem
5 hits

26.3
1 B2C	3 B2B	5 B2C
2 B2G	4 B2G	6 B2C

27.1 1e, 2f, 3d, 4a, 5b, 6a, 7c

27.2 1e, 2d, 3a, 4f, 5b, 6c

27.3
1 indirect cost	4 overhead
2 fixed cost	5 variable cost
3 COGS	6 direct cost

27.4
1 140 korunas	3 25%
2 100 korunas	4 20%

28.1
1 chairs, armchairs, dining tables
2 chairs
3 stools
4 coffee tables
5 chairs
6 stools

28.2
1 overspending	5 underspending
2 spend	6 budget for
3 over budget	7 spending/expenditure
4 under budget	

28.3 1c, 2a, 3b

29.1 2, 1, 7, 5, 8, 4, 6, 3

29.2
1 Cash flow	4 discount
2 upfront	5 credit policy, payment terms
3 trade credit	

29.3
1 key accounts	4 Inland Revenue
2 debtors	5 bad debts
3 creditors	6 write them off

30.1
1 fixed assets	5 current asset
2 current assets	6 not an asset
3 fixed asset	7 intangible asset
4 not an asset	8 not an asset

30.2
1 written off	4 depreciation
2 amortized	5 write down
3 charge, book value	

30.3   **1** false   **2** true   **3** true

31.1

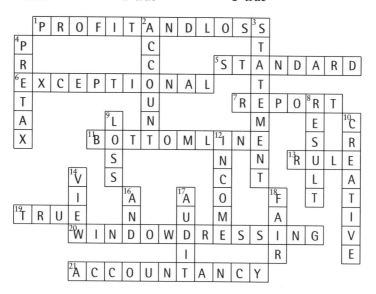

32.1   **1** capital   **6** Lenders
       2 shareholders   **7** loan capital
       3 dividends   **8** principal
       4 equity   **9** interest
       5 lenders   **10** indebtedness

32.2   **1** loan capital, borrowing
       2 collateral, security
       3 gearing, leverage
       4 highly geared, highly leveraged
       5 overleveraged

33.1   1f, 2e, 3b, 4a, 5d, 6c

33.2   **1** collapse, burden   **4** bailout, crisis
       2 repayment   **5** turning, ailing
       3 recovery

33.3   **1** administration   **5** wind up
       2 protection   **6** ceases trading
       3 creditors   **7** liquidation
       4 goes into receivership

34.1   1b, 2c, 3d, 4e, 5a

34.2   **1** bids   **4** predators, prey
       2 restructuring   **5** GS wants to make acquisitions.
       3 hostile bid   **6** merger

34.3
1 diversified
2 subsidiaries
3 parent company
4 divestment
5 restructuring
6 disposes of
7 non-core assets
8 core activities

35.1
| 1 false | 3 true | 5 false | 7 true |
| 2 false | 4 true | 6 true | 8 false |

35.2
1 transfer, current account, an overdraft
2 account balance
3 interest rate
4 interest
5 bank statement, banking charge

35.3 1b, 2c, 3a

36.1
1 brokers
2 traders
3 speculators
4 Wall Street
5 centres
6 institutions
7 City
8 Square Mile

36.2
| 1 true | 3 false | 5 true |
| 2 true | 4 false | |

36.3
1 securities house
2 futures contract
3 commodities
4 currencies
5 commercial paper
6 bonds
7 securities
8 a commodities exchange
9 derivatives

37.1
1 Hong Kong
2 Nikkei
3 New York
4 Dow
5 Nasdaq
6 London
7 CAC 40
8 Dax

37.2
1 blue chips
2 trading
3 very high turnover
4 spectacular gains
5 bull market
6 bullish
7 record high
8 barrier

37.3
1 declines
2 bear, collapse
3 low
4 bearish
5 panic selling
6 rally
7 wiped

38.1
1 economical
2 uneconomical
3 high finance
4 finances
5 finance
6 economics
7 uneconomical

38.2

1	trade deficit	6	balance of trade
2	trade gap	7	inflation rate
3	exports	8	inflation
4	imports	9	out of work
5	trade surplus	10	jobless

38.3

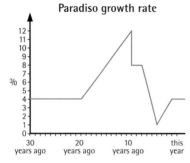

Paradiso growth rate

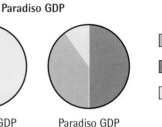

Paradiso GDP

Paradiso GDP
30 years ago

Paradiso GDP
this year

services
industry
agriculture

39.1

1 false	3 true	5 true	7 true
2 true	4 false	6 false	8 true

39.2

Crossword:

1. DEPRESSION
5. PEAK
9. LEVELS OFF
11. BOTTOMS OUT

Down answers shown in grid: RECESSION, SLUMP, STAGFLATION, STAGNATION, STEADY, BOOM, DOWNTURN, NEGATIVE GROWTH, etc.

40.1

1. price fixing
2. market rigging
3. sleaze
4. insider dealing, insider trading; use Chinese walls
5. bribes, backhanders, kickbacks, sweeteners; corruption, sleaze

40.2

embezzlement, embezzler, embezzles, embezzlement, embezzled
faking, faker, fakes, a fake, faked
forgery, forger, forges, a forgery, forged
fraud, fraudster, defrauds, a fraud, fraudulent
money laundering, money launderer, launders money
racketeering, racketeer, racketeers

41.1

1	ethics	4	code of ethics
2	unethically	5	Ethical
3	unethical		

41.2

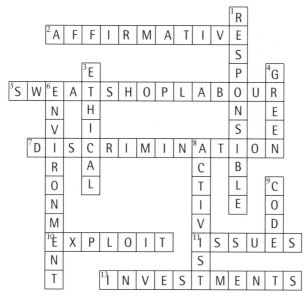

Crossword:
- 2 across: AFFIRMATIVE
- 1 down: RESP... (RESPONS...)
- 5 across: SWEATSHOPLABOUR
- 3 down: ETHICAL
- 4 down: GREEN
- 6 down: ENV...
- 7 across: DISCRIMINATION
- 8 down: ACTIVE / ...
- 9 down: COD...
- 10 across: EXPLOIT
- 11 across: ISSUES
- 13 across: INVESTMENTS

42.1

1 lead time	4 overlapped	7 stage/phase/step/task
2 time	5 make up	8 delays
3 longer than planned	6 schedule	9 downtime

42.2

2 You should avoid interruptions.
3 You should avoid distractions.
4 You shouldn't aim for perfectionism when it's not necessary.
5 You should plan your day in advance.
6 You should go on a time management course.

43.1 4, 1, 2, 5, 3

43.2

1 lifestyle	5 treadmill
2 quality time	6 rat race
3 rebalancing	7 quality of life
4 downshifter's	

44.1 1e, 2c, 3d, 4b, 5g, 6a, 7f

44.2

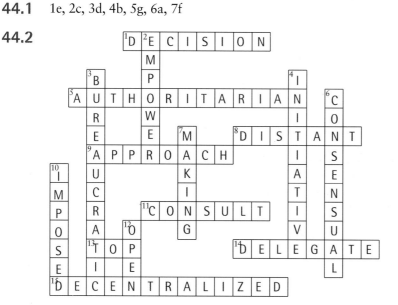

Crossword:
- 1 across: DECISION
- 2 down: EMPOWERE...
- 3 down: BUREAUCRATIC
- 5 across: AUTHORITARIAN
- 4 down: INITIATIV...
- 6 down: CONSENSUS
- 7 down: MAKING
- 8 across: DISTANT
- 9 across: APPROACH
- 10 down: IMPOSE
- 11 across: CONSULT
- 12 down: OPE...
- 13 across: TOP
- 14 across: DELEGATE
- 15 across: DECENTRALIZED

45.1
1 macho culture
2 canteen culture
3 long-hours culture
4 company/corporate culture
5 macho culture
6 long-hours culture

45.2
1a ABC   2a SBC   3a ABC
1b SBC   2b ABC   3b SBC

46.1
1 false   3 false   5 false   7 true
2 false   4 true   6 true

46.2
1 Gammaria   3 Deltatonia
2 Betatania   4 Alphaland

47.1
1 Gammaria   3 Deltatonia
2 Betatania   4 Alphaland

47.2
1 ✗   3 ✓   5 ✗   7 ✓
2 ✗   4 ✓   6 ✗

47.3
1d, 2g, 3c, 4h, 5b, 6f, 7a, 8e

48.1
1 pager
2 mobile phone
3 cordless
4 videophone
5 webcam
6 public telephone

48.2
1 It would be good to see Anna soon. I'll phone her and see when she's free.
2 correct
3 Why don't you ring Pizza Palace and order some takeaway pizza?
4 I rang them five minutes ago but there was no answer.
5 correct
6 correct
7 I'll give her a bell and we'll fix up a meeting.
8 When you get some news, give me a buzz.

48.3
2 four-zero-seven eight-two-four four-three-two-one

3 two-one-three nine-five-six one-seven-double-seven

4 two-one-zero double-two-five one-three-nine-one

5 nine-zero-one double-three-two double-three-double-two

6 five-two-zero six-three-eight two-six-two-six

48.4
1 reservations line
2 helpline
3 hotline
4 information line
5 freephone number

49.1
1b, 2a, 3e, 4b, 5c, 6f, 7d

49.2
1, 5, 3, 6, 7, 2, 8, 4

49.3 Hi James, this is Annelise calling from Sprenger Verlag in Hamburg. It's very difficult to get hold of you. I phoned you earlier, but your switchboard put me through to the wrong extension. Anyway, I'm calling you to discuss the contract we were talking about in Frankfurt. I'll call again later or perhaps you'd like to ring me here in Hamburg on 00 49 40 789 1357. Bye for now.

50.1 1
A: Can I speak to Mrs Lee, please?
B: Speaking. I'm rather tied up at the moment.
A: Sven Nyman here. I'm calling about your order.
B: I wonder if you could call back later.

2
A: Is that James Cassidy?
B: No, I'm afraid not. Can I ask who's calling?
A: Annelise Schmidt. Is James Cassidy available?
B: I'm afraid he's in a meeting. Would you like to leave a message?
A: Could you ask him to call me back as soon as possible?

50.2 This is a suggested answer, but you can use any word beginning with each appropriate letter.
2 V for Victor, A for Alpha, L for Lima, L for Lima, A for Alpha, D for Delta, O for Oscar, L for Lima, I for India, D for Delta
3 W for Whisky, E for Echo, B for Bravo, B for Bravo, E for Echo, R for Romeo
4 WWW dot, britishcouncil all as one word dot, org slash courses
5 P for Papa, E for Echo, T for Tango, E for Echo, R for Romeo, new word, H for Hotel, O for Oscar, U for Uniform, S for Sierra, E for Echo
6 M for Mike, A for Alpha, C for Charlie, P for Papa, H for Hotel, E for Echo, R for Romeo, S for Sugar, O for Oscar, N for November
7 john hyphen smith at cambridge dot ac dot UK

50.3 1g, 2d, 3b, 4f, 5c, 6e, 7a, 8h

51.1 f, b, j, a, h, d, k, e, i, c, g

51.2
1 natural	4 strange
2 strange	5 natural
3 natural	

51.3 1e, 2c, 3b, 4a, 5d

52.1 1 Can you fax your most exciting designs?
2 Sure, I'll fax you the drawings.
3 What's your fax number?
4 Can you fax me the designs our customers will be most interested in?
5 I'll fax them to you straightaway.
6 If you could fax everything, that would be great!

52.2 1 intended recipients, advise, sender
2 confidential, destroy
3 cover sheet, illegible

52.3
1 resent
2 went through
3 did not get stuck
4 did not jam
5 send, through
6 legible

53.1
1 bcc
2 forward
3 reply to all
4 attach
5 send and receive
6 delete

53.2
1 copy Chris Jones in on
2 Attached
3 attachment
4 forwarding
5 Best wishes

53.3
1 AFAIK
2 HTH

54.1
1 arranged/fixed/set up
2 attend
3 put back/postponed
4 brought it forward
5 chaired
6 missed

54.2
1 shareholders' AGM
2 brainstorming
3 department meeting
4 meeting with suppliers
5 chat
6 meeting with a customer
7 project meeting
8 EGM
9 board meeting

54.3   3, 6, 5, 1, 4, 2

55.1
1 Circulate the agenda well in advance
2 venue
3 make their point
4 tactfully
5 minute-taker
6 timetable
7 digress
8 on time

55.2   1b, 2a, 3d, 4c, 5e, 6g, 7f

56.1 1 It's about time we got started.
2 Let's begin, shall we?
3 correct
4 Let's make a start.
5 Let's get down to business.
6 I've called this meeting to ...
7 correct
8 The main objective is to ...
9 As you are aware ...

56.2 1 John, would you like to kick off?
2 Kay, would you like to open the discussion?
3 Len, perhaps you'd like to get the ball rolling?
4 Monica, what do you think?
5 Nigel, what are your views on this?
6 Olive, what are your feelings on this?

56.3 1c, 2a, 3b, 4e, 5d

57.1

¹C			²L		³D	⁴I	S	A	G	R	E	E
O			O		M						
U			S		P		⁵A		⁶P		

Crossword answers: DISAGREE, DIFFERENCE OF OPINION, TEMPER, CALM, ARGUMENT, PROVE; down words: COUGHS, LOSS, DIMPLIGHT, DISCUSS, TEMPO(?), ARGUE, POINT

57.2 1e, 2c, 3b, 4g, 5a, 6d, 7f, 8h

57.3 1c, 2i, 3b, 4j, 5g, 6a, 7h, 8d

58.1 A: If I can just stop you there, you have to admit things were different then. That was in the 1980s.
B: I understand what you're saying, but that's not so long ago. The pressures were the same.
C: To go back to what I was just saying, there are limits as to what we can ask from the creatives. They ...
B: Sorry to interrupt you, but I hate that word 'creative'. A lot of them haven't created anything except chaos since they arrived in the company.
C: Are you implying that the creative department has people who shouldn't be there?

58.2 4, 6, 5, 1, 2, 3

59.1
1 demonstration
2 lecture
3 workshop
4 seminar
5 press conference
6 talk
7 briefing
8 product launch

59.2 1d, 2c, 3a, 4j, 5i, 6e, 7h, 8f, 9b, 10g

60.1 1f, 2c, 3e, 4h, 5g, 6d, 7a

60.2
1 OK. To begin, let's look at the most basic product in our range.
2 Of course, related to the product specifications of our basic model is the issue of product performance.
3 But I'm digressing: let's get back to the product specifications themselves.
4 That's all I have time for on product specifications. Let's move on to our mid-range model.
5 As you can see on this transparency, there are two key features I want to talk about in relation to our mid-range model.
6 I think that covers everything on our mid-range model.
7 Time is moving on, so let's turn to our top-of-the-range product.

61.1
1 smiling
2 eye contact
3 visual aids
4 transparencies
5 flipchart
6 overhead projector, computer screen projector
7 overhead projector, computer screen projector
8 gestures
9 handouts
10 mannerisms

61.2 1d, 2c, 3a, 4b, 5f, 6e

62.1
1 wage negotiations
2 trade dispute
3 trade negotiations
4 labour dispute
5 contract dispute
6 merger negotiations
7 customer–supplier negotiations

62.2 1c, 2f, 3a, 4e, 5h, 6d, 7b, 8g

63.1 1f, 2e, 3b, 4c, 5d, 6a

63.2 3, 6, 4, 2, 1, 5

63.3
1 attitude to time, relationship building
2 relationship building
3 conversational rules
4 hierarchy
5 physical contact
6 conversational rules

64.1 1b, 2c, 3d, 4f, 5e, 6a

64.2 2 As long as engine performance improves by ten per cent, then we may offer a price of $550,000 per unit.
3 On condition that you deliver 20 engines by May, then we will be able to consider a more flexible price.
4 Supposing that you provide good technical support, then we might be able to increase our order.
5 Provided that you supply documentation in Portuguese, we could consider sending our personnel to you for training.
6 Providing that this contract works out OK, we might agree to work with you in future.

64.3 1 horse-trading   4 concessions
2 trade-off   5 haggle
3 gesture

65.1 1 The company were negotiating from strength. They had more bargaining power.
2 The union were negotiating from weakness.
3 The union made demands for a pay increase of 100 per cent, but then they backed down/climbed down.
4 The miners gave in and went back to work.
5 The company had been confrontational and adversarial.

65.2 1b, 2a, 3d, 4e, 5c

65.3 1e, 2c, 3d, 4b, 5a

66.1 1 true   3 true   5 true   7 false
2 false   4 false   6 false

66.2 1 binding
2 commercial
3 binding/legal
4 oral/verbal
5 employment

66.3 1, 6, 5, 7, 4, 8, 3, 2

Index

*The numbers in the index are **Unit** numbers not page numbers.*

bricks-and-mortar /ˌbrɪks ən ˈmɔːtə/ 26

briefing /ˈbriːfɪŋ/ 59

bring to a close /ˌbrɪŋ tuː ə ˈkləʊz/ 58

broke down /ˌbrəʊk ˈdaʊn/ 66

brokers /ˈbrəʊkəz/ 36

budget /ˈbʌdʒɪt/ 28

bugs /bʌgz/ 14

building societies /ˈbɪldɪŋ səˌsaɪətiz/ 12

building society /ˈbɪldɪŋ səˌsaɪəti/ 35

bull market /ˈbʊl ˌmɑːkɪt/ 37

bullet point /ˈbʊlɪt pɔɪnt/ 60

bullish /ˈbʊlɪʃ/ 37

bully /ˈbʊli/ 8

bureaucratic /ˌbjʊərəˈkrætɪk/ 11, 44

burned out /ˌbɜːnd ˈaʊt/ 43

burnout /ˈbɜːnaʊt/ 43

business /ˈbɪznɪs/ 10, 11, 18, 26, 47

business process re-engineering (BPR) /ˌbɪznɪs ˌprəʊses riː endʒɪˈnɪərɪŋ/ 18

business-to-business (B2B) /ˈbɪznɪs tə ˈbɪznɪs/ 26

business-to-consumer (B2C) /ˈbɪznɪs tə kənˈsjuːmə/ 26

business-to-government (B2G) /ˈbɪznɪs tə ˈgʌvənmənt/ 26

busy tone /ˈbɪzi təʊn/ 49

buyer /ˈbaɪə/ 19

buying managers /ˈbaɪɪŋ ˌmænɪdʒəʳz/ 19

CADCAM 14, 16

calendar /ˈkæləndə/ 42

call /kɔːl/ 48

call centres /kɔːl ˌsentəz/ 24

call someone's bluff /ˌkɔːl ˌsʌmwʌnz ˈblʌf/ 65

call back /ˌkɔːl ˈbæk/ 49

candidate /ˈkændɪdət/ 3

canteen culture /kænˈtiːn ˌkʌltʃə/ 45

capacity /kəˈpæsəti/ 16

capital /ˈkæpɪtəl/ 17

captains of industry /ˌkæptɪnz əv ˈɪndəstri/ 10

car/automobiles /kɑːr ˈɔːtəməʊbiːlz/ 13

cards /kɑːdz/ 59

career ladder /kəˈrɪə ˌlædəʳ/ 7

career paths /kəˈrɪə pɑːðz/ 7

cash /kæʃ/ 28, 29, 33

cash cows /ˈkæʃ kaʊz/ 28

cash mountain /ˈkæʃ maʊntɪn/ 33

cash pile /ˈkæʃ paɪl/ 33

cash reserves /ˈkæʃ rɪˌzɜːvz/ 33

cashflow /ˈkæʃfləʊ/ 29

casual Fridays /ˌkæʒuəl ˈfraɪdeɪz/ 46

casually /ˈkæʒuəli/ 46

catalog /ˈkætəlɒg/ 22

catalogue /ˈkætəlɒg/ 22

catering /ˈkeɪtərɪŋ/ 13

cc /ˌsiːˈsiː/ 53

cease trading /ˌsiːs ˈtreɪdɪŋ/ 33

cellphone /ˈselfəʊn/ 48

cellular /ˈseljələ/ 48

cellular phone /ˌseljələ ˈfəʊn/ 48

chain store /ˈtʃeɪn stɔː/ 24

chairperson /ˈtʃeəˌpɜːsən/ 55

challenging /ˈtʃælɪndʒɪŋ/ 43

change hands /ˌtʃeɪndʒ ˈhændz/ 37

charge /tʃɑːdʒ/ 23, 30

charisma /kəˈrɪzmə/ 44

charities /ˈtʃærɪtiz/ 12

cheap /tʃiːp/ 23

cheque /tʃek/ 35

cheque account /ˈtʃek əˌkaʊnt/ 35

chief executive officer (CEO) /ˌtʃiːf ɪgˌzekjətɪv ˈɒfɪsə/ 9

chief financial officer /ˌtʃiːf faɪˈnæntʃəl ɒfɪsə/ 9

chief operating officer /ˌtʃiːf ˈɒpəreɪtɪŋ ɒfɪsə/ 9

Chinese walls /ˌtʃaɪniːz ˈwɔːlz/ 40

churn out /ˌtʃɜːn ˈaʊt/ 16

circulate /ˈsɜːkjəleɪt/ 55

classified advertisements /ˌklæsɪfaɪd ədˈvɜːtɪsmənts/ 25

clicks-and-mortar /ˌklɪks ən ˈmɔːtəʳ/ 26

client base /ˈklaɪənt beɪs/ 19

clientele /ˌkliːɒnˈtel/ 19

clients /ˈklaɪənts/ 19

climb down /ˈklaɪm daʊn/ 65

clinching a deal /ˌklɪntʃɪŋ ə ˈdiːl/ 66

clock in /klɒkˈɪn/ 2

clock off /klɒkˈɒf/ 2

clock on /klɒkˈɒn/ 2

clock out /klɒk aʊt/ 2

closing a deal /ˌkləʊzɪŋ ə diːl/ 66

code of conduct /ˌkəʊd əv ˈkɒndʌkt/ 41

code of ethics /kəʊd əv ˈeθɪks/ 41

cold calls /ˌkəʊld ˈkɔːlz/ 24

collapse /kəˈlæps/ 33, 37

collateral /kəˈlætərəl/ 32

combine /kɒmˈbaɪn/ 34

come to a consensus /ˌkʌm tuː ə kənˈsensəs/ 58

commercial /kəˈmɜːʃəl/ 11, 36

commercial airline /kəˌmɜːʃəl ˈeəlaɪn/ 11

commercial artist /kəˌmɜːʃəl ˈɑːtɪst/ 11

commercial disaster /kəˌmɜːʃəl dɪˈzɑːstə/ 11

commercial land /kəˌmɜːʃəl ˈlænd/ 11

commercial paper /kəˌmɜːʃəl ˈpeɪpə/ 36

commercial television /kəˌmɜːʃəl ˌteliˈvɪʒən/ 11

commission /kəˈmɪʃən/ 5

commodities /kəˈmɒdətiz/ 36

commodities exchange /kəˈmɒdətiz ɪksˈtʃeɪndʒ/ 36

common ground /ˌkɒmən ˈgraʊnd/ 65

commute /kəˈmjuːt/ 2

commuters /kəˈmjuːtəz/ 2

company /ˈkʌmpəni/ 11, 45

company car /ˌkʌmpəniˈkɑː/ 5

company hierarchy /ˌkʌmpəni ˈhaɪərɑːki/ 7

company pension scheme /ˌkʌmpəni ˈpentʃən skiːm/ 35

compensation /ˌkɒmpənˈseɪʃən/ 5

compensation package /ˌkɒmpənˈseɪʃən ˌpækɪdʒ/ 5

compensation payment /ˌkɒmpənˈseɪʃən ˌpeɪmənt/ 5

compete /kəmˈpiːt/ 20

competition /ˌkɒmpəˈtɪʃən/ 20

competitions /ˌkɒmpəˈtɪʃənz/ 25

competitors /kəmˈpetɪtəʳz/ 20

hang up /'hæŋ ʌp/ 49
harass /'hærəs hə'ræs/ 8
hard /hɑːd/ 2
head /hed/ 9
head office /hed 'ɒfɪs/ 6
headhunt /'hedhʌnt/ 3
headhunter /'hedhʌntə/ 3
headhunting /'hedhʌntɪŋ/ 3
headquarters (HQ)
/ˌhedˈkwɔːtəz -ˈ-/ 6
health and safety inspectors
/ˌhelθ ən 'seɪfti ɪnˌspektəz/ 8
health and safety issues /ˌhelθ
ən 'seɪfti ˌɪʃuːz/ 8
healthcare /'helθkeər/ 13
heavy industries /ˌhevi
'ɪndəstriz/ 13
hedging /'hedʒɪŋ/ 58
helpline /'helplaɪn/ 48
hi-tech /ˌhaɪ'tek/ 15
hierarchical /ˌhaɪə'rɑːkɪkəl/ 45
high finance /haɪ 'faɪnæns/ 38
high-end /haɪ'end/ 23
high-priced /haɪ'praɪst/ 23
high-street banks /ˌhaɪ striːt
'bæŋks/ 35
highly geared /haɪli 'ɡɪəd/ 32
highly leveraged /haɪli
'liːvərɪdʒd/ 32
hire /'haɪə/ 3
hiring /'haɪərɪŋ/ 3
hits /hɪts/ 26
hold shares /həʊld'ʃeəz/ 32
holiday /'hɒlədeɪ/ 47
horse-trading /'hɔːs treɪdɪŋ/ 64
hospitality /ˌhɒspɪ'tæləti/ 47
hostile bid /ˌhɒstaɪl'bɪd/ 34
hotline /'hɒtlaɪn/ 48
household goods /ˌhaʊshəʊld
'ɡʊdz / 13
HTH 53
human resource management
(HRM) /ˌhjuːmən 'rɪzɔːs
ˌmænɪdʒmənt/ 6
human resources (HR)
/ˌhjuːmən rɪ'zɔːsɪz/ 6
human resources department
(HRD) /ˌhjuːmən 'rɪzɔːsɪz
dɪˌpɑːtmənt/ 6
humour /'hjuːmə/ 47
hypermarket /'haɪpəˌmɑːkɪt/
24
icons /'aɪkɒnz/ 53
impasse /'æmpæs/ 66

impolite /ˌɪmpə'laɪt/ 57
imports /'ɪmpɔːts/ 38
imposed /ɪm'pəʊzd/ 44
in charge of /ɪn 'tʃɑːdʒ əv/ 1
in parallel /ɪn 'pærəlel/ 42
in stock /ɪn stɒk/ 17
in the black /ɪn ðə 'blæk/ 35
in the red /ɪn ðə 'red/ 31
in-house /ɪn'haʊs/ 4, 7, 17
in-house training /ɪnˌhaʊs
'treɪnɪŋ/ 4
income statement /'ɪŋkʌm
ˌsteɪtmənt/ 31
incorporated/Inc
/ɪn'kɔːpəreɪtɪd/ 12
indebtedness /ɪn'detɪdnəs/ 32
index /'ɪndeks/ 37
indexes /'ɪndeksɪz/ 37
indices /'ɪndɪsiːz/ 37
indirect costs /ˌɪndɪrekt 'kɒsts/
27
industrial /ɪn'dʌstriəl/ 6
industrial action /ɪnˌdʌstriəl
'ækʃən/ 6
industrial robots /ɪnˌdʌstriəl
'rəʊbɒts/ 16
industrial scale /ɪnˌdʌstriəl
'skeɪl/ 14
industrialize /ɪn'dʌstriəlaɪz/ 13
industry /'ɪndəstri/ 13
inflation rate /ɪn'fleɪʃən reɪt/
38
inflationary /ɪn'fleɪʃənəri/ 38
information line /ˌɪnfə'meɪʃən
laɪn/ 48
initiative /ɪ'nɪʃətɪv/ 44
inland revenue /ˌɪnlənd
'revənjuː/ 29
innovate /'ɪnəveɪt/ 15
innovative /'ɪnəvətɪv/ 15
inputs /'ɪnpʊts/ 17
insider dealing /ɪnˌsaɪdə 'diːlɪŋ/
40
insider trading /ɪnˌsaɪdə
'treɪdɪŋ/ 40
insolvent /ɪn'sɒlvənt/ 33
intangible assets /ɪnˌtændʒəbl
'æsets/ 30
intellectual property
/ˌɪntəlektjuəl 'prɒpəti/ 15
intense /ɪn'tens/ 20
interest /'ɪntrəst/ 32, 34, 35
internet access /'ɪntənet ˌækses/
26

internet banking /ˌɪntənet
'bæŋkɪŋ/ 35
internet service provider(ISP)
/ˌɪntənet 'sɜːvɪs prəˌvaɪdə/
26
interruptions /ˌɪntə'rʌpʃənz/ 42
interviews /'ɪntəvjuːz/ 3
introduce /ˌɪntrə'djuːs/ 59
invent /ɪn'vent/ 15
inventories /'ɪnvəntriz/ 17
invest /ɪn'vest/ 32
investment companies
/ɪn'vestmənt ˌkʌmpəniz/ 35
investors /ɪn'vestəz/ 32, 36
invoice /'ɪnvɔɪs/ 29
invoicing /'ɪnvɔɪsɪŋ/ 29
irreconcilable differences
/ˌɪrekənsaɪləbl 'dɪfərənsɪz/
66
issue /'ɪʃuː/ 66
issued /'ɪʃuːd/ 36
issues /'ɪʃuːz/ 41
job insecurity /ˌdʒɒb
ɪnsɪ'kjʊərəti/ 7
job title /'dʒɒb taɪtl/ 46
jobless /'dʒɒbləs/ 38
join /dʒɔɪn/ 3
joint account /ˌdʒɔɪnt ə'kaʊnt/
35
joint venture /ˌdʒɔɪnt 'ventʃə/
34
jump /dʒʌmp/ 39
junk mail /'dʒʌŋk meɪl/ 24
just-in-time /ˌdʒʌstɪn'taɪm/ 17
kaizen /kaɪ'zen/ 18
keep calm /ˌkiːp 'kɑːm/ 57
keep things moving /ˌkiːp θɪŋz
'muːvɪŋ/ 54
key accounts /kiː ə'kaʊnts / 29
key players /kiː 'pleɪəz/ 20
keypad /'kiːpæd/ 49
kick off /kɪk 'ɒf/ 56, 63
kickback /'kɪkbæk/ 40
knowledge /'nɒlɪdʒ/ 17
laboratories /lə'bɒrətəriz/ 14,
15
labour-intensive /ˌleɪbə
ɪn'tentsɪv/ 16
labour/labor /'leɪbə/ 6, 17, 41,
60
labour/labor unions /'leɪbə
ˌjuːnjənz/ 6
last mile problem /ˌlɑːst maɪl
'prɒbləm/ 26

money spinners /ˈmʌni ˌspɪnəz/ 28

monotone /ˈmɒnətəʊn/ 60

mortgage /ˈmɔːgɪdʒ/ 35

motivated /ˈməʊtɪveɪtɪd/ 4

multimedia presentation /ˌmʌltiˈmiːdiə ˌprezənˈteɪʃən/ 60

multinational /ˌmʌtiˈnæʃənəl/ 11

mutual /ˈmjuːtʃuəl/ 12, 35, 62

mutual advantage /ˌmjuːtʃuəl ədˈvɑːntɪdʒ/ 62

mutual funds /ˌmjuːtʃuəl ˈfʌndz/ 35

mystery shoppers /ˌmɪstəri ˈʃɒpəz/ 18

nationalized /ˈnæʃənəlaɪzd/ 11

needs /niːdz/ 63

negative growth /ˌnegətɪv ˈgrəʊθ/ 39

negotiate /nɪˈgəʊʃieɪt/ 62

negotiating /nɪˈgəʊʃieɪtɪŋ/ 63, 65

negotiations /nɪˌgəʊʃiˈeɪʃənz/ 62

negotiator /nɪˈgəʊʃieɪtə/ 62

neon signs /ˌniːɒn ˈsaɪnz/ 25

nervous breakdown /ˈnɜːvəs ˈbreɪkdaʊn/ 43

net margin /ˌnet ˈmɑːdʒɪn/ 27

net profit /ˌnet ˈprɒfɪt/ 31

niche market /ˌniːʃ ˈmɑːkɪt/ 23

night shift /ˈnaɪt ʃɪft/ 2

nine-to-five job /naɪn tə faɪv ˈdʒɒb/ 2

non-core assets /ˌnɒn kɔː ˈæsets/ 34

non-executive directors /nɒn ɪgˌzekjətɪv dɪˈrektəz/ 9

non-negotiable /nɒn nɪˈgəʊʃiəbl/ 65

non-profit organizations /nɒn ˌprɒfɪt ˌɔːgənaɪˈzeɪʃənz/ 12

not-for-profit organizations /nɒt fɔː ˈprɒfɪt ˌɔːgənaɪˌzeɪʃənz/ 12

numerate /ˈnjuːmərət/ 4

objective /əbˈdʒektɪv/ 56, 63

obsolete /ˈɒbsəliːt/ 15

obstacles /ˈɒbstəklz/ 65

offer /ˈɒfə/ 3, 64

office worker /ˈɒfɪs wɜːkə/ 2

offices /ˈɒfɪsɪz/ 6

on neutral ground /ɒn ˌnjuːtrəl ˈgraʊnd / 63

on schedule /ɒn ˈʃedjuːl/ 42

open /ˈəʊpən/ 44

open-plan offices /ˌəʊpən ˈplæn ˌɒfɪsɪz/ 6

operator /ˈɒpəreɪtə/ 49

options contract /ˈɒpʃənz ˌkɒntrækt/ 36

order /ˈɔːdə/ 29

organized /ˈɔːgənaɪzd/ 4

original concept /əˈrɪdʒənəl ˈkɒnsept/ 14

out of work /ˌaʊt əv ˈwɜːk/ 38

outline /ˈaʊtlaɪn/ 59

outplacement /ˈaʊtˌpleɪsmənt/ 7

outside suppliers /ˌaʊtsaɪd səˈplaɪəz/ 17

outsource /ˈaʊtsɔːs/ 7

outsourcing /ˈaʊtsɔːsɪŋ/ 17

outstanding /ˌaʊtˈstændɪŋ/ 66

over budget /ˌəʊvə ˈbʌdʒɪt/ 28

overdraft /ˈəʊvədrɑːft/ 35

overhead costs /ˈəʊvəhed ˌkɒsts/ 27

overhead projector (OHP) /ˌəʊvəhed prəʊˈdʒektə/ 60

overheads /ˈəʊvəhedz/ 27

overlap /ˈəʊvəlæp/ 42

overleveraged /əʊvə ˈliːverɪdʒd/ 32

overproduction /ˌəʊvəprəˈdʌkʃən/ 16

overspent /ˌəʊvəˈspent/ 28

overtime /ˈəʊvətaɪm/ 5, 6

overwhelmed /ˌəʊvəˈwelmd/ 43

overwork /əʊvəˈwɜːk/ 43

owe /əʊ/ 29

own-brand product /əʊnˈbrænd ˌprɒdʌkt/ 22

own-label product /əʊn ˈleɪbəl ˌprɒdʌkt/ 22

packaging /ˈpækɪdʒɪŋ/ 21

page views /peɪdʒ ˈvjuːz/ 26

pager /ˈpeɪdʒə/ 48

panic selling /ˈpænɪk selɪŋ/ 37

paper qualifications /ˈpeɪpə ˌkwɒlɪfɪˈkeɪʃənz/ 4

parent company /ˈpeərənt ˌkɒmpəni/ 34

part-time job /ˌpɑːt taɪm ˈdʒɒb/ 1

part-time work /ˌpɑːt taɪm ˈwɜːk/ 1

partners /ˈpɑːtnəz/ 17

partnership /ˈpɑːtnəʃɪp/ 12

parts /pɑːts/ 17

password /ˈpɑːswɜːd/ 26

patents /ˈpeɪtənts/ 15

pay /peɪ/ 5

pay off /ˈpeɪ ɒf/ 35

payables /ˈpeɪəblz/ 29

payment terms /ˈpeɪmənt tɜːmz/ 29

payphone /ˈpeɪfəʊn/ 48

payroll /ˈpeɪrəʊl/ 6

peak /piːk/ 39

penalties /ˈpenəltiz/ 42

penetrate a market /ˌpenɪtreɪt ə ˈmɑːkɪt/ 20

pension /ˈpenʃən/ 5, 35

perfectionism /pəˈfekʃənɪzəm/ 42

performance /pəˈfɔːməns/ 5, 7, 18

performance reviews /pəˈfɔːməns rɪˌvjuːz/ 7

performance-related bonuses /pəˌfɔːməns rɪˌleɪtɪd ˈbəʊnəsɪz/ 5

perks /pɜːks/ 5

permanent /ˈpɜːmənənt/ 1

personal organizers /ˈpɜːsənəl ˈɔːgənaɪzəz/ 42

personnel /ˌpɜːsəˈnel/ 6

personnel department /ˌpɜːsəˈnel dɪˌpɑːtmənt/ 6

pharmaceuticals /ˌfɑːməˈsjuːtɪkəlz/ 13

phase /feɪz/ 42

phone /fəʊn/ 48

phonecard /ˈfəʊnkɑːd/ 48

physical contact /ˌfɪzɪkəl ˈkɒntækt/ 47

physical delivery /ˌfɪzɪkəl dɪˈlɪvəri/ 26

pitch /pɪtʃ/ 60

place /pleɪs/ 21

place an order /ˌpleɪs ən ˈɔːdə/ 29

plastic /ˈplæstɪk/ 35

plummet /ˈplʌmɪt/ 39

poison pill /ˈpɔɪzən ˌpɪl/ 34

position /pəˈzɪʃən/ 3

post /pəʊst/ 3

postpone /pəʊstˈpəʊn/ 65

remuneration /rɪˌmjuːnəˈreɪʃən/ 5

remuneration package /rɪˌmjuːnəˈreɪʃən ˈpækɪdʒ/ 5

repetitive /rɪˈpetətɪv/ 2

repetitive strain injury (RSI) /rɪˌpetətɪv ˈstreɪn ˌɪndʒəri/ 8

reply /rɪˈplaɪ/ 49, 53

reports /rɪˈpɔːts/ 31

representatives /ˌreprɪˈzentətɪvz/ 63

research and development (R&D) /rɪˈsɜːtʃ ən dɪˈveləpmənt/ 15

research centre/center /rɪˈsɜːtʃ ˌsentə/ 15

researchers /rɪˈsɜːtʃəz/ 14

reseller /riːˈselə/ 24

resend /riːˈsend/ 52

resign /rɪˈzaɪn/ 7

resolution /ˌrezəˈluːʃən/ 66

resolve /rɪˈzɒlv/ 55

responsibility /rɪˌspɒnsəˈbɪləti/ 1

responsible for /rɪˈspɒnsəbl fɔː/ 1

restructure /ˌriːˈstrʌktʃə/ 7

restructuring /ˌriːˈstrʌktʃərɪŋ/ 34

result /rɪˈzʌlt/ 28, 31

retail /ˈriːteɪl/ 13, 24

retail outlet /ˈriːteɪl ˌaʊtlət/ 24

retailers /ˈriːteɪləz/ 24

retained earnings /rɪteɪnd ˈɜːnɪŋz/ 33

retire /rɪˈtaɪə/ 7

retirement /rɪˈtaɪəmənt/ 7

return your call /rɪtɜːn jɔː ˈkɔːl/ 49

revenue /ˈrevənjuː/ 27

rewarding /rɪˈwɔːdɪŋ/ 43

reworking /ˌriːˈwɜːkɪŋ/ 18

right first time /ˌraɪt ˌfɜːst ˈtaɪm/ 18

ring /rɪŋ/ 48

rival /ˈraɪvəl/ 20

role of silence /rəʊl əv ˈsaɪləns/ 47

rollout /ˈrəʊlaʊt/ 14

round of negotiations /ˌraʊnd əv nɪˌɡəʊʃiˈeɪʃənz/ 62

routine /ruːˈtiːn/ 2

royalties /ˈrɔɪəltiz/ 15

rude /ruːd/ 57

rules of conversation /ˌruːlz əv kɒnvəˈseɪʃən/ 47

run /rʌn/ 1

run out of time /rʌn aʊt əv ˈtaɪm/ 58

run over /rʌn ˈəʊvə/ 60

sack /sæk/ 7

safe /seɪf/ 14

salary /ˈsæləri/ 5

sale /seɪl/ 27

sale price per unit /ˌseɪl praɪs pɜː ˈjuːnɪt/ 28

sales areas/sales territories /ˈseɪlz ˌeəriəz/ˈseɪlz ˌterɪtəriz/ 25

sales figures /ˈˌseɪlz ˌfɪɡəz/ 27

sales forecast /seɪlz ˌfɔːkɑːst/ 27

sales forecasts /ˈseɪlz ˌfɔːkɑːsts/ 14

sales growth /ˈseɪlz ɡrəʊθ/ 27

sales manager /ˈseɪlz mænɪdʒə/ 25

sales meeting /ˈseɪlz miːtɪŋ/ 27

sales outlet /ˈseɪlz aʊtlet/ 24

sales team /ˈseɪlz tiːm/ 27

salesforce /ˈseɪlzfɔːs/ 25

salesmen /ˈseɪlzmən/ 25

salespeople /ˈseɪlzpiːpl/ 25

saleswomen /ˈseɪlzwɪmɪn/ 25

satisfying /ˈsætɪsfaɪɪŋ/ 2

savings account /ˈseɪvɪŋz əkaʊnt/ 35

scam /skæm/ 40

schedule /ˈʃedjuːl/ 42

screen /skriːn/ 60

search engine /ˈsɜːtʃ endʒɪn/ 26

seating plan /ˈsiːtɪŋ plæn/ 59

secondly /ˈsekəndli/ 60

securely /sɪˈkjʊəli/ 26

securities /sɪˈkjʊərətiz/ 36

security /sɪˈkjʊərəti/ 26, 32, 36

selection process /sɪˈlekʃən prəʊses/ 3

self-driven /ˌself ˈdrɪvən/ 4

self-employed /ˌself ɪmˈplɔɪd/ 11, 12

self-motivated /ˌself ˈməʊtɪveɪtɪd/ 4

self-starters /self ˈstɑːtəz/ 4

seller /ˈselə/ 19

seminar /ˈsemɪnɑː/ 59

send an email /ˌsend ən ˈiːmeɪl/ 53

senior /ˈsiːniə/ 7, 46

senior executive /ˌsiːniə ɪɡˈzekjətɪv/ 9

service industries /ˈsɜːvɪs ɪndəstriz/ 13

service sector /ˈsɜːvɪs sektə/ 13

services /ˈsɜːvɪsɪz/ 13, 19

settle disputes /ˌsetl dɪˈspjuːts/ 62

settlement /ˈsetlmənt/ 66

severance package /ˈsevərəns pækɪdʒ/ 5

severance payment /ˈsevərəns peɪmənt/ 5

sex discrimination /seks dɪˌskrɪmɪˈneɪʃən/ 8, 41

sexual harassment /ˌsekʃuəl həˈræsmənt/ 8

share capital /ˌʃeə ˌkæpɪtəl/ 32

share options /ˈʃeə ɒpʃənz/ 5

share price /ˈʃeə praɪs/ 37

shareholders /ˈʃeəˌhəʊldəz/ 32

shares /ʃeəz/ 36

shift /ʃɪft/ 2

ship /ʃɪp/ 29

shop /ʃɒp/ 24

shopping cart /ˈʃɒpɪŋ kɑːt/ 26

shopping centre /ˈʃɒpɪŋ sentə/ 24

shopping malls /ˈʃɒpɪŋ mɔːlz/ 24

shopping precinct /ˈʃɒpɪŋ priːsɪŋkt/ 24

shortage /ˈʃɔːtɪdʒ/ 16

shortlist /ˈʃɔːtlɪst/ 3

show off /ʃəʊ ˈɒf/ 54

sick /sɪk/ 33

simultaneous /ˌsɪməlˈteɪniəs/ 42

site /saɪt/ 6, 26

situation /ˌsɪtjuˈeɪʃən/ 3

situations vacant /ˌsɪtjueɪʃənz ˈveɪkənt/ 3

skill /skɪl/ 4

skilled /skɪld/ 4

skyrocket /ˈskaɪˌrɒkɪt/ 39

slash /slæʃ/ 39

sleaze /sliːz/ 40

slide projector /ˈslaɪd prəʊdʒektə/ 60

slump /slʌmp/ 39

small investors /smɔːl ɪnˈvestəz/ 35

small or medium-sized enterprise (SME) /ˌsmɔːl ɔː ˌmiːdiəm saɪzd 'entəpraɪz/ 11

small talk /'smɔːl tɔːk/ 63

smart casual /ˌsmɑːt 'kæʒjuəl/ 46

smile /smaɪl/ 60

snowed under /snəʊd 'ʌndə/ 51

soar /sɔː/ 39

socially responsible /ˌsəʊʃəli rɪ'spɒnsəbl/ 41

sole owner /ˌsəʊl'əʊnə/ 12

sole proprietor /ˌsəʊl prə'praɪətə/ 12

sole trader /ˌsəʊl'treɪdə/ 12

sophisticated /sə'fɪstɪkeɪtɪd/ 23

special displays /ˌspeʃəl dɪ'spleɪz/ 25

special offers /ˌspeʃəl 'ɒfəz/ 25

specifications/specs /ˌspesɪfɪ'keɪʃənz/speks/ 18

speculator /'spekjəleɪtə/ 36

spend /spend/ 28

sponsor /'spɒnsə/ 25

sponsorship /'spɒntsəʃɪp/ 25

spot checks /ˌspɒt 'tʃeks/ 18

stable /'steɪbl/ 39

staff /stɑːf/ 6

stage /steɪdʒ/ 42

stagflation /stæg'fleɪʃən/ 39

stagnation /stæg'neɪʃən/ 39

stalemate /'steɪlmeɪt/ 66

stand-up presentation /stænd ʌp ˌprezən'teɪʃən/ 59

start-ups /'stɑːtʌps/ 10

state pension /ˌsteɪt 'penʃən/ 35

state-of-the-art /ˌsteɪt əv ði ɑːt/ 15

state-owned /ˌsteɪt əʊnd 'kʌmpəniz/ companies 11

steel /stiːl/ 13

step /step/ 42

stereotypes /'steriəʊtaɪps/ 45

sticking points /'stɪkɪŋ pɔɪnts/ 65

stiff /stɪf/ 20

stimulating /'stɪmjəleɪtɪŋ/ 2, 43

stock exchange /'stɒk ɪks,tʃeɪndʒ/ 36

stock market /'stɒk mɑːkɪt/ 36

stock options /'stɒk ɒpʃənz/ 5

stocks /stɒks/ 17

stoppage /'stɒpɪdʒ/ 6

store /stɔː/ 24

stored /stɔːd/ 17

street furniture /'striːt ˌfɜːnɪtʃə/ 25

street vendors /'striːt vendərz/ 19

stress-induced /'stres ɪndjuːst/ 43

stressed out /ˌstrest 'aʊt/ 43

stresses and strains /ˌstresɪz ənd 'streɪnz/ 43

stressful /'stresfʊl/ 43

stretched /stretʃt/ 43

strike /straɪk/ 6

structure /'strʌktʃə/ 59

subcontracting /'sʌbkən,træktɪŋ/ 17

subordinates /sə'bɔːdənəts/ 44

subsidiaries /səb'sɪdiəriz/ 34

sum up /sʌm 'ʌp/ 58, 60

supermarket /'suːpə,mɑːkɪt/ 24

suppliers /sə'plaɪəz/ 17

support staff /sə'pɔːt stɑːf/ 6

surf /sɜːf/ 26

surge /sɜːdʒ/ 39

surveys /'sɜːveɪz/ 14

sweatshop labor /ˌswetʃɒp 'leɪbə/ 41

sweetener /'swiːtənə/ 40

switchboard /'swɪtʃbɔːd/ 49

systematic /ˌsɪstə'mætɪk/ 4

tactfully /'tæktfəli/ 55

takeover /'teɪkəʊvə/ 34

talented /'tæləntɪd/ 4

talk /tɔːk/ 59

target /'tɑːgɪt/ 24, 27

task /tɑːsk/ 42

team of equals /ˌtiːm əv 'iːkwəlz/ 45

team-players /ˌtiːm'pleɪəz/ 4

technical support /ˌteknɪkəl sə'pɔːt/ 6

technology /tek'nɒlədʒi/ 15

telecommunications /ˌtelɪkə,mjuːnɪ'keɪʃənz/ 13

telecommuting /ˌtelɪkə'mjuːtɪŋ/ 2

telemarketing /ˌtelɪ'mɑːkɪtɪŋ/ 24

telephone banking /ˌtelɪfəʊn 'bæŋkɪŋ/ 35

teleworking /'telɪwɜːkɪŋ/ 2

temporary /'tempərəri/ 1, 7

terminate /'tɜːmɪneɪt/ 7

testing /'testɪŋ/ 14

textiles /'tekstaɪlz/ 13

the City /ðə 'sɪti/ 36

the close /ðə kləʊz/ 37

the four ps /ðə fɔː 'piːz/ 21

the free market /ðə ˌfriː 'mɑːkɪt/ 19

the market /ðə 'mɑːkɪt/ 19

the Square Mile /ðə skweə 'maɪl/ 36

threats /θrets/ 65

time /taɪm/ 42

time is money /ˌtaɪm ɪz 'mʌni/ 42

time management /ˌtaɪm 'mænɪdʒmənt/ 42

timeframe /'taɪmfreɪm/ 42

timescale /'taɪmskeɪl/ 42

timetable /'taɪm,teɪbl/ 42, 63

timings /'taɪmɪŋz/ 60

tips /tɪps/ 5

tiring /taɪəɪŋ/ 2

to license /tə 'laɪsəns/ 15

to market /tə 'mɑːkɪt/ 21

to rally /tə 'ræli/ 37

to recover /tə rɪ'kʌvə/ 37

to settle /tə 'setl/ 66

toll-free number /ˌtəʊl,friː 'nʌmbə/

top-down approach /tɒp'daʊn əprəʊtʃ/ 44

top-end /tɒp'end/ 23

total costs /ˌtəʊtəl'kɒsts/ 27

total market capitalization /təʊtəl ˌmɑːkɪt ˌkæpɪtəlaɪ'zeɪʃən/ 37

total quality management (TQM) /ˌtəʊtəl ˌkwɒləti 'mænɪdʒmənt/ 18

tough /tʌf/ 2, 20

tourism /'tʊərɪzəm/ 13

trade balance /treɪd 'bæləns/ 38

trade credit /treɪd 'kredɪt/ 29

trade deficit /treɪd 'defɪsɪt/ 38

trade down /treɪd 'daʊn/ 23

trade gap /'treɪd gæp/ 38

trade surplus /treɪd 'sɜːpləs/ 38

trade unions /treɪd 'juːnjənz/ 6

trade up /treɪd 'ʌp/ 23

tradeoff /'treɪdɒf/ 64

traders /'treɪdəz/ 36

trading /'treɪdɪŋ/ 37

traditional retailing /trədɪʃənəl 'riːteɪlɪŋ/ 26

train /treɪn/ 4

Acknowledgements

The author would like to thank Sally Searby, Bernie Hayden, Rachel Harrison and the team at Cambridge University Press for smoothly guiding the book through the editorial process.

The author and publishers would like to thank the following students and teachers who reviewed this edition and gave us invaluable feedback which helped to shape the material.

Jacqueline Harding, Madrid, Spain; Ann Claypole, Birkenfeld, Germany; Yvette Petitjean, Brussels, Belgium; Kristi Alcouffe, Bonelles, France; Philippa-Louise Dralet, Paris, France; Aedin Whitty, Amsterdam, Holland; Joseph Peacock, Warsaw, Poland; Rachel Tomlinson, Stroud, UK; Students at OISE, Cambridge.

The publisher would like to thank the following for permission to reproduce photographs and artwork.

Illustrators: Clinton Banbury: pages 37, 74, 101, 118, 130; Adrian Barclay: page 122; Kathy Baxendale: pages 60, 128, 130, 134; Beccy Blake: page 18; Gecko Ltd: pages 20, 22, 24, 43, 49, 56, 60, 64, 68, 72, 82, 85, 100, 104, 105, 110, 137, 139. 141, 146, 152; Gary Wing: page 54.

Photographs: Art Directors and Trip: pages 55, 78, 92*l*, 112*r*; Camera Press: pages 29 *tl*, *bl*, 32, 34*l*, 66*l*; Getty Stone Images: pages 10, 11, 12*l*, 28*l*, 40*l*, 52*r*, 58*tl*, 81*l*, 90, 94*t*, 96; Impact Photos: pages 95, 102*m*; Katz Pictures: page 126*t*; Network Photographers: pages 16, 34*m*, 83, 102*b*; Pictor International: pages 17, 20, 23, 36*b*, 42*b*, 62, 73, 98*r*, 102*t*, 117*r*, 127*tl*, 135; Popperfoto: pages 29 *tr*, *tm*, *br*, 138; Powerstock Zefa: page 80; Retna: page 29 *bm*; Rex Features: pages 34*r*, 58*br*; Robert Harding Picture Library: pages 28, 46, 52*l*, 66*r*, 81*r*, 83, 94*b*, 112*l*, 117*m*, 140; Roland Harris: pages 12*r*; Ronald Grant Archive: page 58; Telegraph Colour Library: pages 40*r*, 58*tr*, 92*t*, 98*l*, 117*l*, 120, 127*r*; Topham Picturepoint: page 57; Sally and Richard Greenhill: page 36*t*.

Cover design by John Dunne.

Design and page layout by Gecko Ltd.